SHO-GA-NAI

A Time In America When The Music Stopped

1941 - 1946

Written by

Fil Kae

Pu ko'o Moloka'i

Edited by

Mary Maier

Revised June 19, 2016

BEGINNINGS

Aloha. Hi, I'm MIYAKO, but you can call me KITTY. Am from Hilo, on the big island of Hawai'i, in da Hawaiian Islands.

The first thing I remember when things started for me was asking Mom how old I was and where I was born.

"You are almost three now. You were born at Tutu Louisa's house on the tenth of December, nineteen thirty five."

"Tutu" is Hawaiian for aunt. She was the family's closest friend, a widowed Hawaiian woman who was also a midwife. I stayed with Tutu Louisa when our family worked during the daytime.

My parents were Kama'aina, that means "child of the land". They had lived in the Islands since the late 1800's. Most of our ancestors came from Japan and the Ryukyus (Okinawa), and also San Francisco. My ancestral knowledge is incomplete beyond that, as it is with many families in Hawai'i. I am told that is typical.

Grandmother, *Sobosan*, was from Na'a on the great island of Okinawa, in the Ryukyus, a Japanese prefecture. My Grandfather was from the mainland, he was of mixed heritage. Most of the family was American citizens except Grandmother, she came too late, because of immigrant restrictions.

I was almost four when my sister, Tomiko, picked me up from Tutu Louisa's house after her school and told me on our way home that I was to be sent to the mainland, San Francisco.

My parents had four children. Two brothers, Eichi, the oldest, and Michio. Then my sister, Tomiko. They were all two years apart. I came along six years after my sister. The family called me "da kid came lately."

We lived in two old plantation houses near Hilo. They were very small, that is why we were able to rent two of them. Trouble was they were very old and run down, but that was all my parents could afford. Before I was born, my parents had worked in the fields. I never learned much about what they did, except that they did not care for the work. Long, hard and very exhausting hours with very low wages and very abusive field supervisors called "lunas." The lunas were not Hawaiians, but mainland southerners who kept to the traditions of plantation paternalism. They attempted to control the workers' lives, such as limiting wage spending to their "company store", and prohibiting island workers from speaking any language other than their dialect of English.

"Why do I havta go to San Francisco? Ha'kum jes me? Why no one else go?" I asked Tomiko.

"You go with Granpa," she said. "Mom say we will have better chances of getting work in San Francisco. She say Dad will have a good chance to work with Granpa. He has found a home that will be big enough for da whole family.

"Mom say it won't be bad. Granma is already expecting you for now. She is fixing up da new house. Then all of us can live together. It will really be great."

Then when Mom came home from work I asked her, "Why jes me an Papa?" We all called our Grandfather, "Papa."

"Because of schools an dakine," she say. "Right now we can only afford to send you. Your brothers and sister are in the middle of their schooling and work, so are needed to help the family here. Your Grandmother will be expecting you. It will have to be soon since your Grandfather must return and you will be going with him. I'm sorry, Kitty, we could not tell you sooner. We will all miss you for just a little while. It will be in a few days after your birthday in December."

As far as I could remember, I was always called "Kitty." It was not until later did I learn I had a formal name, Miyako. When I found out, I really did not know what to think. I have always been little and my *Sobosan*, Grandma, had said when I was just a toddler that "she is so small and quiet and is just like a little kitten." So before I ever had a chance, or was old enough to object, I was stuck with the nickname of "Kitty." But that's OK. As far as I could remember I would often formally call her *Sobosan*, Japanese, for Grandmother. It was practically the only Japanese word I knew for a long time. I also was, like Grandma said, kinda smaller den other kids my age. I still am, but I won't ever say much about that.

The year was nearly 1939. Everyone worked, even my brothers and sister when not at school. I was raised partly by my aunty and Grandma. At that time, Sobosan had left for San Francisco to join my Grandpa. He was successful in forming a business he had worked hard to build. At that time, Hawai'i was still suffering economically from the Great Depression while the rest of the U. S. was slowly recovering. Our family was having a tough time getting by.

The day before I was to go, I again asked them, "Mom, Dad, can't I not go? Gonna miss dis place, even if I not hava bedroom. Dis is where I was born. Even if everyone says that Kilauea is so fierce and big, an madam Pele might rumble and things get really scary, am not afraid no more. I'm four now. Not a baby. "

Mom cried and said, "Don't worry, we will all be coming very soon and then you can have your own bedroom and we will be together in one house, our family home. Someday you will be able to return. I hear San Francisco is very nice and beautiful. Your Grandmother writes to say how wonderful it is, you will be surprised. She is waiting for you."

All the way to the boat in Hilo harbor I cried. They got me some presents, including a little suitcase. All my friends and the family were there to wish me goodbye, but that did not matter. I still not want to go and did not stop crying.

Papa helped me onto the inter-island boat. It was sadness, so sad all the way to Honolulu where the ship was that would take us to San Francisco. I did not even care when Papa pointed out Maui and Moloka'i, the islands we passed on the way to O'ahu. I could never forget that picture in my mind of the family waving at me from the

Hilo waterfront and Mouna Kea looking down on everything.

Honolulu was, much bigger than Hilo and very noisy, so many people. We stayed at a little hotel for one night.

That night, Papa tried to calm me as I was still so sad and cried when I thought of my home and Hilo.

"Please Kitty, I know how sad you are, but you are going to our first real home. We can all live in a house together. Try to think about the new home when we leave tomorrow."

In the early morning, we were taken to Honolulu harbor.

"Papa, is it… that great big white ship?" I spied it docked in the harbor.

"No, that is the tourist steamer from the mainland. We will be on a smaller one, a freighter. It carries cargo, but also passengers."

Ours was still very big compared to the inter-island ship we had taken from Hilo. From where I stood on the wharf looking up at it, it was still very high and scary. I did not know how we would get aboard.

Papa pointed to a long and steep ladder with steps that he called a "gangplank." He motioned to me to begin climbing up it as he followed. I started up, but hesitated. To me it was very long, narrow, steep and scary. Looking up, I became dizzy and frightened. I turned around, retreated behind him, holding on tight to his legs, I cried.

Then someone lifted me and before I knew it I was on the ship.

"Thank the nice mate, Kitty!" said Papa.

The man who lifted me up was a sailor who worked on the freighter. I forget his name now. He was very big and very quiet. Until we reached San Francisco, he would frequently talk to me, knowing I had never been on a ship before. He took me around and showed me various decks and many compartments. I'll not forget him. That whole trip really took away most of my sadness from leaving home. We went almost everywhere on the ship. For instance, the engine room where he said the "black gang" worked. They were boiler workers, where in the old days the coal they used made them and everything black.

That engine room was just a little scary, the noise of those big engines, you could not hear anything else but that scary roar.

I liked best just to lean over the railings and stare at the waves. Colors of blue, green, mixed with the white ocean foam and sprays reminded me of where we lived.

Remembering still made me sad, but I tried each day to think about our new home in San Francisco. Mostly it was easy when I thought about how we all had to share the little old stuffy houses where we had to stay. I kept asking Papa to tell me more about our new real-home. He must have grown tired of me asking and told me to just imagine. It started getting easier to sleep at night. The ship also rocked back-n-forth all the time. I really liked that, it made me happy. I enjoyed watching the waves lap against the ship and rise up and down as we traveled. I loved the way it swayed, it helped me sleep and reminded me of home. I hoped that there would be boats in San Francisco we could sail on.

One day, I discovered some fish that seemed to be swimming along with the ship, but they were a lot faster than us and would even jump out of the water. They were much different than I had ever seen before. I even saw some big sea birds that visited the ship. Someday I want to return to Hawai'i on such a ship. even though I heard that now ya havta only fly. Not seem fair.

On the day that we were about to arrive in San Francisco Papa took me way forward to the very bow of the ship, called the "fo'c'sle" (a mariner term). It was really exciting, except when I looked way down where the bow sliced through the water making great waves. The ship cutting the water in two. It was scary. I held tight, afraid I was going to fall.

I saw something bumpy on the horizon. "Look, it's California," Papa said, pointing to the first little bit of land we could see.

As I stared, it gradually grew nearer and larger and seemed to divide and spread and we sailed right between the hills as they grew.

There was a strange line that ran between them. As we got closer I could see it was a bridge. Not like the little ones in Hilo. It was huge and kept growing bigger and more frightening. I thought our ship was going to hit it.

"Papa, what is that big bridge?" I asked.

"Oh Kitty, that's the brand new Golden Gate Bridge."

I held on to him, thinking we would crash into it. But we went under it. I got dizzy looking up at it. It was really too big and way too high. It seemed like a long time that I just stared up at it, and could not say anything.

Just beyond the bridge were really big buildings. Very tall, and larger than those even in Honolulu. Everything was wonderful, but big and frightening all at the same time.

"Is that San Francisco?"

"Yes, Kitty, that's the City."

Before I knew it we had arrived in the harbor at a wharf bigger than our ship. It was time for us to leave.

"Come Kitty, we are in San Francisco," he said. But I hesitated on stepping on that steep gangplank. Then I saw Grandma standing on the dock looking up and waving at us.

"*Sobosan!*" I yelled and waved. She waved back and smiled. I was so excited to see her, I started running down the gangplank to where she stood, forgetting how steep and scary it was. When I stepped onto the dock she picked me up and we hugged. She looked wonderful and happy. We kinda cried together.

"Oh my Kitty, you look so happy. Did you enjoy your trip?"

I told her about everybody I met. How the ship's crew complimented me because I never got seasick. Then I cried again, I so was missing everybody in Hilo, even if Papa kept cheering me up and the trip was fun and exciting.

"I saw the big bridge! How did they make it so large and so high?"

Some friends of my grandparents drove us from the harbor through all the hills and streets until we reached the west side of the City and to what was to become our home. By that time, I had fallen asleep even though I wanted to see every big building and steep hill and all the trees in the big park they all talked about. It was all so exciting. I dreamt about the bridge and later kept asking to visit it time and time again.

I awoke in my new home. It was a lot bigger than any place I had ever been. I spent a lot of time exploring each floor. The ceilings seemed really high. Not like those low ones at home that Eichi and Dad would bump. The walls had wood paneling, the windows were tall, and the floors had shiny wood with different designs. Grandma said that the house was a Victorian design. It was old, built in the late last century. The house faced west toward the ocean. At the front of it were lots of steps leading up to a nice big front door, with woodcarving and a bell visitors could ring. I got in trouble ringing. It made a wonderful musical sound. The front door is actually on the second floor because the front steps leading from the sidewalk were very high and steep. They were almost too high for me to step. It was a while before I could climb them.

There were two floors above that floor and one below. It opened out onto a nice backyard. The house was so much nicer than anything I ever lived in or even visited in Hilo. I really felt proud and happy. It would be so great for the whole family. And I slept in my own bed for the very first time in my whole life. It was first hard to get to sleep. Staring up at the ceiling with its big dark wooden beams and longing for everyone to come and stay, I was happy.

Papa asked me to help in the back yard to build a garden. It took us a long time because we built a winding rock path from the house to a little teahouse. We had to travel many places for rocks, plants, trees and grass seeds. The yard was bare in the beginning. Later we visited the big park and got so many ideas that it was difficult deciding what we had to do. I helped him for the rest of that year and into the next, planting grass, trees, bushes and patches of flowers. I hoped that we could get some palms like we had in Hawai'i, as well as other Island trees, bushes and flowers. Papa actually built a little teahouse, made wind chimes and even found rocks and gravel for the walks. I made a little rock and shell garden. It included shells I had collected on the beach on the Island of Hawai'i.

We got a lot of our ideas from the big park called Golden Gate. It was so big, seemed to go forever and I didn't know how long it would be before I ever saw the whole park, maybe never.

My grandparents sometimes took me along with their friends to visit downtown. All the winding streets, big buildings, trolleys, and stores. I had to hold on to someone so I would not get lost. Always I would get so tired of seeing so much that I was glad when we returned home. One day we drove over the Golden Gate Bridge. It was so exciting and so different from the first time I saw it from the ship. The wind blowing fog and clouds from the ocean right across the bridge road, it was scary. I was overwhelmed all over again. I asked too many questions for everyone to answer. They finally promised to show me books and magazines from the library to try and quiet me.

As exciting a time it all was, I still kept thinking about Hawai'i and felt homesick.

Papa worked down town with his business partners. Grandma also worked with Papa part time. They purchased a new gramophone. They had brought the family's collection of music records from Hawaii, Japan and the mainland. I was happy because I had missed our music and was delighted to listen to many records I had never heard before. Music had always been so much a part of our family.

When it came to one thing, Grandma was sorta strict. She didn't mind that I spoke pidgin like the kids I grew up with in the neighborhood, but she insisted that I should learn regular English. So I would be prepared when I started attending school and be able to talk to the neighborhood kids where we now lived. I did have a little trouble when I started playing with new kids. They were all friendly and welcomed me, but I knew quickly that often they did not understand dakine pidgin I spoke.

They had me use a desk in their room. It was only just for studying. Papa used it when worked at home with his calligraphy, mostly hiragana. I was not a good student and really did not know why I had to learn English. I was stubborn. Of course when I began to meet neighborhood kids I noticed that I had some trouble. Some said I talked 'funny', but no one really complained. Grandma also insisted I start learning arithmetic and practice my reading and writing.

Back home, Tomiko had already started very early helping me read and write. Mom, Dad and Grandma had taught my brothers and Tomiko earlier.

The neighborhood was really different. With rows of houses very close together on each side of the street. Kids played between the houses and in the streets, which was sometimes scary because cars came by and we had to run for the sidewalks. The neighbors were really nice. One neighbor had come from Italy, the Desparis', they were always having us over to dinner and we all visited each other.

It was slow getting used to some foods in the City. I missed many foods from the Islands. Especially poi, which I had eaten almost daily since I was a baby. It is mixed, for instance, with fish or eaten by itself. Poi is made from the taro root or "kalo" as the Hawaiians say. It grows in shallow ponds or dry soil. We used to pick it for Aunty Louisa to cook into poi or bake up from the raw root. I also missed papaya and bananas. They were available daily from our yards. Unfortunately papaya had to be imported and was expensive. The good apple variety bananas are difficult to find in stores. Grandma spent a lot of time searching for them. The variety in the stores are imported from large Latin American plantations. They taste awful and at first are hard to get used to.

I was able to go to school when I was four and a half. Because my birth was in December (1935) I started in early 1940. Thanks to Grandma and the family I already had some reading, writing and arithmetic, but my pidgin still made some speaking tough for a while. I got used to the teachers' English and they got used to my say, or something like that, just a little bit, dakine is sometimes baffling to them.

My first couple weeks in school were not very good on my grandparents. I was real trouble. The first day I attended school, Kindergarten, with all the other new kids. It seemed all right but I really was bored. In the afternoon when lunch was over and everyone went outside to play, instead of returning to class, I left. Finding my own way back home. I remembered the way, it was no trouble. Even crossing several streets and one busy boulevard. No one was home so I managed to get in the backyard and eventually into the house. When my grandparents arrived I was in serious trouble.

"Why are you home so early?" Grandma asked me. She had a very big mean frown.

"There was nothing to do there, so after lunch I came home. I was bored. There was nothing to read or write. The teacher read something I already knew and we did some messy water colors. I remember how to get home. I was very careful and came right back here. Did I do something wrong?"

What I didn't understand was that my teacher and my Grandparents were in trouble. I was even then a truant. I had a difficult time understanding what school was all about. So, on that first day I found I was almost a criminal. Having broken a law or something like that. It was frightening. I had never had someone so mad at me. I just wanted to go back to Hawai'i. I even thought a little while of what streets to take to run away. First to town, then the harbor, then get a ship going back home.

Finally, after what seemed like a difficult time, I understood and returned to school, realizing ultimately that no one was really very mad at me. I knew that they loved me and were seriously worried for a while.

My brothers and sister came in the autumn of 1940 and my parents a little later. I shared a bedroom with Tomiko. My brothers shared another and my parents the remainder. It was finally done. We were all in the same house for the first time. I was happy to sorta show them around the house, and the neighborhood and our garden. I had really missed Mom, Dad, my sister and brothers. It was wonderful to have everybody together. I took Tomiko to my school because she had to register special that first day. She was starting the fifth grade. I was in the second half of kindergarten. The school was north from our house, about five blocks.

I was so glad to see Tomiko. I had really missed her. She was bigger and older, by six years, but we were always close. She looked out for me and kept me safe from bullies. I was very much smaller for my age than other kids. An ongoing frustration of mine that is just part of my life, I guess. When we would compare our heights with a mark on one kitchen wall, I complained that when I reached age 4 she was much taller for that age. I just never caught up with her. Had to get used to that.

It was nice to see Michio my youngest brother, he is three years older than Tomiko. Very noisy, but smart. Of course, there is brother Eichi. He is the biggest guy in the family, even bigger than Dad. I used to think he got some of my height by accident. I used to tell him that he should not have stolen it from me. He would laugh and so would I. I liked to kid with him. I was really proud of having such a brother so big. He was quiet and thought a lot before he said anything. I could never do that. I just talked and said sometimes the wrong thing. But mostly he was not annoyed when he had to bend way over to listen when I talked. Until much older I had such a little small voice. Some people complained, but I did not like shouting.

Michio enrolled in the junior high and Eichi enrolled in the junior college in the City. He wanted to study history and was very interested in legal studies. He planned to later take some college courses in law or teaching if he could qualify.

I remember that there was a World's Fair just before the rest of the family came. It was held, mostly at a place called Treasure Island between the City and the East Bay cities, just off the middle of the Bay Bridge. That bridge also was newer and really big.

Lots of neighbors used to tell me how they still liked to use the ferries instead of that bridge to travel east. Everyone where we lived seemed to always call San Francisco the "City". I think it was that they were so proud of it.

One interesting memory was when visiting the harbor and embarcadero and noticing that a lot of fishing and bigger ships were flying little American flags above Japanese and other foreign flags. Dad explained that because they were visiting in American waters they were required to carry our flags.

In early 1941, I started the first grade. It was nice having had already read and done some writing earlier than most kids in school. But my biggest trouble still was, of course, English. My pidgin mostly remained. It is hard to change.

In the summer of 1941, my Grandfather passed away. It was really tough on the entire family. We loved him so much. Helping us during the Depression in Hawai'i and in San Francisco. The new house was the greatest help because he was born in San Francisco and his family had helped him buy the house. He had a mixed mainland and Hawaiian background. I still miss him. I got so close to him when we built the back yard garden and being with him when we traveled all that way from Hawai'i. I am still lonely without him.

BIRTHDAY

In early December, my teacher called me to her desk and told me I was to give the Pledge of Allegiance for all of the first three grades, and Kindergarten, on a special day. It would also be my birthday and I would get a little party afterward.

"Well Kitty, you have certainly improved your English and some of your speech. We have all become used to your pidgin, and you are an excellent student. We are very proud of you," my teacher, Miss Gregory said.

"Gee thanks, I hope it don't matter that I have to raise my voice a lot when I say dakine Pledge before the classes?"

"No, you will be on the platform in the primary auditorium."

"Well, OK an thanks, am gonna work really hard on it."

"Tomiko, guess what? I get to give the Pledge before all the early grades, an you can come."

"Oh Kitty, that will be great, I know you can do it. We will be proud, the family. Now we gotta get going so we are not late. I'll help you with everything."

That weekend before my birthday, I mostly did not sleep, so excited. Starting that Friday, we all had so much to do. Mom and Granma got the dress material and pattern from the Montgomery Ward catalogue I found. I helped them all weekend. I even got to do a little sewing on the dress. It was very hard, but they seemed to make dakine look easy. The colors were yellow and some kind of light brown trim. Mom said it was beige and went well with me because I still have a nice tan from the Islands. It was my first real dress.

On Saturday, my brothers and sister took us to town. I saw my first movie that was all in color, Fantasia. It was full of wonderful music. I recognized some music we used to hear on records and the radio, but never in a movie and I had never seen animation. It made the music and my memories so different. I liked it so much that I kept asking everyone if we could see it again. My brothers left, but Tomiko stayed at the theatre and I was allowed to watch and listen to everything twice. Afterward, we took a couple buses home. The music and animation stuck in my mind for the whole weekend and more. The music and visions kept playing in my mind.

On Sunday, the 7th, Pearl Harbor in Honolulu was bombed which made us very mad at the Japanese because for us it was very personal. Being Kama'ainas ('born there") and hapa (part Hawaiian), we resented the attack and were shocked and now worried. Eichi kept mentioning that now our nation was going to be at war with Japan and possibly its partners (called Axis) Italy and Germany. I did not really understand much at that time about such matters.

Dad was worried after the attack because my sister Tomiko and I might have a problem when we returned to school on Monday. I did not understand. I still had to finish some of the ironing of my clothes and get washed and ready for the following day.

When I finally fell asleep I was just thinking about the movie and the excitement of giving the Pledge. I kept looking at my new clothes, lunch pail and cleaned-up shoes, then forgot to turn off the lights. Tomiko must have done that when she went to bed after her studies.

Then it was daylight. I could see the time. I looked over and saw that Tomiko was sleeping.

"Tomiko, come on we gotta get up, it's time to eat and get to school, remember?"

"Yes, sure, I remember, how could I forget? You kept reminding me yesterday and last night. Now just calm down so you don't eat your breakfast too fast." She looked at me so funny, at least so I thought.

"Am I funny? Da way you looking at me?"

"No, you look so nice and clean and all those new things everybody made for you."

"Hey, you saying I been dirty or what? An I helped make these things too."

"No, of course not; you just look extra nice on your birthday. Now we better get going. We are riding with Mr. an Mrs. Desparis, they are just leaving, hurry!"

I sure felt excited. Riding in their car was special, even if only just a few blocks to school. I have always liked looking at the City, it's so funny, with most houses all stuck together and some sort of looking like ginger bread, as Mom would say. I even wanted to someday eat one of them kind of breads or whatever they are. The City is so different from Hilo where we had lived in Hawai'i. We were let off just outside the gate.

"It's locked, Kitty," Tomiko said.

"That's OK, I can just squeeze in, but you go an wait or go another way. I'll be OK, see ya later when we all go to the assembly for the Pledge."

"Just be careful, remember what Dad said, that's why I am supposed to go with you. Something might happen because of what happened in Honolulu on Sunday."

"OK, I be careful."

Tomiko went on and I crossed the big yard to the primary courtyard. There was no one there, and I wanted to practice the Pledge again and to try dancing like I remember from the movie, Fantasia. It was so good I told myself. I can still hear the music all the time and want to dance what I saw, but not in front of everyone. Just sort of shy, someone might think I was crazy, because I'm the only one hearing it. I even checked around all the corners of the courtyard, no one was there. When I close my eyes I can still see those fairies and other funny colored animals dancing and so I try to dance too. It was so much fun and beautiful music, the best part of da happy time. Because happy time is forever and ever as I remember. It was just so wonderful to whirl and twirl to the music. Just like remembering when Dad or Granma picked me up and we danced to the music, spinning so much and no one could stop laughing. We all have had such good times with the music.

The courtyard was still quiet and I didn't remember how long I was dancing to the music when I began getting a little dizzy.

Suddenly the music stopped.

I opened my eyes and saw all the kids. Lots of them were looking at me. I felt funny and embarrassed. Wanted to say something, maybe an excuse for being a little dizzy, must have looked funny. That was when I heard them yelling at me. Most were in sort of a circle almost around me, and getting closer and closer. They kept yelling a word at me. I not know why, but started to cry, catch my breath and began shaking. I was afraid. I didn't like that word, but not sure what it was at first, but when I thought I knew I did not understand and just shook my head and tried to smile, but not see anyone smile back. Why? Everyone always smiled back before. They just stared and frowned saying that word again and again. Something made me start to run, but with everyone so close now I tried to get out between two kids. One stopped and pushed me, I pushed back. I think I made her fall. I kept running, but wanted to say I was sorry and not want her to be hurt. Others were hitting me. I wanted to ask them why, but there was no time, just had to run.

Running out of the court, I got to the big yard. Other kids started yelling the same thing at me and running toward me, one pushed me as I ran past him.

"What did I do, what bad did I do?" I said to myself. I had

no breath or voice to speak to them. I could feel my heart pounding.

I was feeling so embarrassed and ashamed. I was not supposed to be running away, but they wouldn't stop yelling at me. And as I ran, I managed once to yell a little at them.

"Please just stop, please!" What had I done wrong? I must be awful bad. But I didn't do anything, honest. I was just trying to dance and hear my music and practice the Pledge.

Now there was no music, it stopped, and my good feelings were gone. I did not realize I had left the schoolyard and the school.

I had been crossing many streets, not even looking for cars, just kept running, tripping, and falling. Then, when I was almost out of breath, I saw the stoplights. The street was very busy and the light was red but I wanted to keep running. I saw a man getting ready to cross as the light turned green. I called to him.

"Hey mister!" He looked back at me as I grabbed his hand. He just smiled and let me cross with him. As soon as we got to the sidewalk again I thanked him and ran. He smiled. I was glad he said nothing about me not being in school or that I was crying, or that I was now very dirty and my dress was torn and I had some scuffs and bruises. That is when I realized that I had forgot my new lunch pale, sweater and homework.

Stopping for that moment, I realized that I was supposed to give the Pledge of Allegiance.

"I did not keep my promise," I said to myself. That was awful bad. They won't let me say it now because of what I had done, being so bad. But what was it? Why? Why? I did not know or if I could return to school, ever.

I kept running and running. Crying so much it was hard to see where I was going or where I was. I made it to our street. Looking at our home, I just stopped. I could not go there, my parents, everyone, would be so disappointed and so mad at me. I could not go anywhere. I had been very bad, and so ashamed.

I remembered I told Tomiko it would be OK. What would she think now? It's my fault and now I was in big trouble, all by myself. Alone. Where was I gonna go? Just standing there still and scared.

I tried to climb the steps to our house and tripped again, fell hard and screamed really awful, I was hurt. I was hurt outside and way way inside too. And I not know why.

For what I thought was a long time, I just laid with my head resting against the door. I was so alone and felt so bad.

Then Granma was holding me, "Oh Miyako, what is the matter? Why are you home?"

"Oh *Sobosan*, what is jap?"

"Da kids, they wouldn't stop calling me that. I ran away, been very bad. Just don't really know why, but am so ashamed. Oh really bad, not know why I ran, just ran and ran. Now I can't give da Pledge, I promised, but not keep. The family is going to be ashamed and mad at me. I must be punished for running away. I left all my things at school. I can't go back, not ever or never."

"Oh no, we are not mad at you, you have done nothing wrong." Granma replied. "It's not what you did, but who they think you are. They are mistaken, they are wrong. We are so sorry we did not talk to you more about what happened Sunday in Honolulu."

"But why did they say that at me? Do they think I'm jap? What they kept yelling at me. Like them guys that bombed and got us into war? I don't understand, that's not me an I'm not them."

"No, of course, you are right, but now it is getting late and we must take you to school. First you need to change your clothes and wash up."

"But Granma, I can't, no, no! Cannot go back, not now. I been so bad. I ran away. Clothes messy and torn, everything is lost. You an Mom worked so hard. How can I do it now? Please not now, I am so ashamed. Awfully sorry, please forgive, please."

"Yes, we forgive you, and you did nothing bad. And yes you can go back. I'm going to be there. We will talk to your teacher and your sister will be nearby."

"But she is not in my class and I did not keep my promise to get her, just ran away. I am so scared now. More awful things will happen."

"Now Kitty, we are going back to school. You are very brave. It will be all right. Now get ready!"

Granma would not hear me when I said I was scared. And kind of yelling at me, but I knew it was OK. When we got to school she was talking to the teacher for a long time. Some of the kids were looking at me and I knew they were angry with me. I was more scared and could not stop shaking. She took me to Miss Gregory who smiled.

"Oh Kitty, we are so glad to see you made it. Everything is going to be all right, just come along."

I stood still and looked back at Granma, she smiled and nodded her head and waved goodbye. That's when I saw Tomiko. She took my hand and with the teacher we went into the little auditorium where the first three grades and kindergarten were all sitting. It was very very quiet there, and everyone was looking at me. Then Miss Gregory told them my name and that I would lead the whole class in the Pledge. Some kids were shaking their heads and looked at me very funny and mean. I just closed my eyes and said it very slowly and really loud so they all could hear.

"Oh Kitty, that was very good," Miss Gregory said. Everyone went to their classes. I opened my eyes, but I was crying and still scared and shaking. She put her hand on my shoulder and helped me into class. Before I could go to my seat she explained that I had been frightened when many kids had thought I was like those Japanese who bombed Pearl Harbor.

"Kitty and her family are Americans, they are citizens from Hawai'i where Pearl Harbor was attacked. She and her family are mostly of Japanese ancestry, having very long ago come from Japan and settled in the Territory of Hawai'i which is a part of the United States of America."

Some kids shook their heads like they were saying that they did not believe the teacher. Lots of kids kept staring at me. I don't think they liked me anymore. That was strange because I don't remember them doing that before. It was sadness. I not wanted anyone to not like me. It made me very very lonely and heartbroken. I wanted to cry. Things were starting to be different. I got my sweater and put it on, was so chilly. My lunch pail was missing so Tomiko took me to the cafeteria to eat. I could not eat much. Everyone there seemed extra quiet. A couple of my friends did smile. We ate alone and she took me back to the classroom. It was hard the rest of the day to think.

I asked Tomiko that afternoon on the way home about our ancestors, "I don't understand, no one ever told me about being ancestor Japanese, that is so strange. How can someone think I'm Japanese? No one ever said that to me. I don't understand. It does not make any sense."

"You know that lots of our grandparents were from Japan and the Ryukyus," she answered. "But some of them are from here too."

"Yeah, but never knew what all that really meant. I'm an American, but Miss Gregory said I am Japanese-American. But how can I be both? We have never been to Japan and now we are at war with them. It's so crazy. Besides I am who I always am and not both. Just American."

Because we are from Hawai'i we are Kama'aina. That

means, children of the aina, which means land. And some say we are Hawaiians also.

"Yes, it's confusing," Tomiko added, "We are now in trouble, our whole family. Like those kids, lots of people do not know any difference. And Kitty, that's really crazy, it's scary."

About halfway home I stopped and told Tomiko, "I just don't understand why? I'm the same person all the time we been in our school. Even before and no one ever said anything to me about being ancestor Japanese, or Japanese-American. I am still just me, like everyone else, an American and a citizen. Just like all of us."

I started crying, it seemed so different. "How come I got to be different now?" I asked her. "How can I look like who I am not? I know I am not bad and am not a Jap. They are bad and I hate them for what they did. I am not them, I am just like all us kids in school, not different."

"Yes, you are not different, Kitty. I am just like you and I don't feel different so don't feel bad. I know everything should have been explained concerning the bombing of Pearl Harbor," Tomiko said, putting her arm around me. We continued home.

When we arrived home, Granma asked how I felt.

"I am ok, thanks for taking me back to school. But I have to talk to you some more because I don't know what to think. I'm just an American, not Japanese. And don't see that I can be 'Japanese-American' like my teacher said we are. I remember hearing about Japanese-Americans but not understand who that was. I can't be both? I never heard that. I don't remember ever anyone was saying or talking about that. It's confusing and I don't think it makes sense being two different peoples at the same time."

She did not answer, only smiled.

That night, when the family settled down to dinner, I told some of what had happened at school.

"After Granma took me back I got to give the Pledge of Allegiance. I was so scared, had closed my eyes all the time and was shaking and sort of crying. Miss Gregory was really nice, but only one of my friends talked to me, another smiled and others gave me funny looks. I could not find my new lunch pail and I had to start my homework book over. Miss Gregory said I didn't have to make up some lessons. She said she understood."

"What about your birthday celebration?" Mom asked.

I didn't know what to say. Everyone was looking at me. My stomach got funny and I wanted to cry.

"Nothing, nothing," I said and ran from the table into the hall and cried. Then Granma came and said something and put her arm on my shoulder.

"Kitty, it's all right, you can tell us some other time if you want. Would you like to just sit?"

I sat with her in the front room on our big chair in the dark and didn't say anything.

No one asked me anything after that about what happened at the party. I did not know how to answer them. Nor did I know what to do. I was very sad and I felt so ashamed and hurt deep down inside. At my party, besides Miss Gregory and me, only one friend came. It was all so quiet because all the other kids stayed away.

Granma had left me alone. I cried myself to sleep.
"Kitty, wake up, I think there is something funny in the kitchen," Tomiko was shaking me.

Everything was dark, but there were flickering lights in the kitchen. She took my hand and led me.

"Surprise, happy birthday!"

Mom, Dad, Eichi, Michio, Granma and Tomiko were waving little lighted candles, it was beautiful. I stood there and cried because I didn't know what to do.

"Oh Mom, Granma, everybody, I not know what to say now. I am sorry for crying. I still feel so ashamed, but you guys make me better."

"Kitty, we all have some presents and some ice cream," Eichi said.

I didn't know what to do. I was so tired. I sat there and ate some ice cream and I started tearing at one nice package, but started crying again and put my head down. I was sleepy. Mom and Dad picked me up.

"That's OK honey, you can open them later, we will save something for you. You have had a very long day. It's all right if you go to bed," Mom said.

Everybody said goodnight.

After that, I sort of forgot about that day. Tomiko walked
to school with me, but it was not easy. Some friends were
only talking to me when we were alone, but no one yelled
at me. It was very lonely at school. I kept thinking
something bad was going to happen.

I talked to Dad and told him I felt different and afraid, but
did not know why, and that I kept dreaming about the kids
and about being at war. I could not sleep.

"Kitty, it is OK, we all have worries to live with.
Remember, all have *gaman,* (which he explained means to
persevere). All the family has worries, but faith that we
will persevere."

"I'll try, Dad, I hope I don't wake up anyone else when I
cry and remember what happened at school," I said.

He looked at me with a big smile. "You can always wake
us up and cry. We have all done that," he said.

"Thanks, Dad, I love you."

A couple days later, we heard that the authorities in
Hawai'i arrested two of our uncles and one aunt. We also
heard about arrests of other Issei, first born Japanese-
Americans, and some Nissei, second born Japanese-
Americans, on all the islands.

The relatives were being held at a military stockade on

Sand Island, near Honolulu, with hundreds of others.

Eichi said that the arrests included very prominent Nisei citizens, as well as all Issei and Japanese visiting and working in Hawai'i. "It's now martial law there, as of the 8th of the month. We don't know much more right now."

He explained that the Hawaiian Islands would remain under martial law, military authority, for most of the war. Eichi also explained that the government considered all Issei to be enemy aliens.

"What about other enemy aliens? Italy and Germany are now at war with us," Michio asked.

"They too are subject to arrest. Eichi said. "What is a little confusing is that all first born Japanese-Americans here in America and in Hawai'i cannot become citizens. That is why they are also considered enemy aliens. But I doubt that they all will be interned because, like Grandma and our relatives, they have broken no laws and are generally not considered a threat to America. Some years ago, the Congress denied all first-born the right to be citizens, our parents and grandparents."

Everyone looked at Grandmother. "I expect I'll be visited by some FBI any day now. I already heard from some of my friends. They are arresting those who are holding important positions in the community. Mine is not, but being also an Issei they likely will come," Granma said.

"You mean someone would really arrest you, Granma?" I asked.

"Well I don't know. I am an Issei and with your Grandfather I was an officer in our little company. But now that he is gone and I am retired, I don't know, it's very complicated."

"Isn't it also complicated because Grandpa was 'Hapa'?" Eichi asked.

"Yes'" she answered. "But I hope it does not come up because he is gone now. Because of his part-American family, he was able to buy this house.

Days later, the government visited the family. It was the FBI.

"Mom! Dad!" Tomiko cried out, we have visitors. Two big men were at the front door. They introduced themselves as the F.B.I.

"Is your boss the one who makes vacuum cleaners?" I asked. That really startled them and the guys looked really cross at me.

"Who said that?" one of them asked.

"Me, Miyako, your boss, is Mr. Hoover, OK?" One looked around and then saw me smiling up at him. He smiled and laughed.

"Well, kid, he is just fine, but he is not that man. We are with the United States government and are here to see Mrs. Higa."

"Oh, that's our granma, but she is Mrs. Issa now," Tomiko corrected the agent.

"But are you not actually related to the notorious Mr. Higa of Okinawa?" he said, speaking to Granma.

"No, I was never related to that man. Higa is my nee name. It is a common name in Okinawa," Granma answered.

"There are other persons of question that we believe you know: Tomo Kitabayashi and Otoku Miyasi of Okinawa and Japan."

"No, I don't even recall such persons. My only relationship was with my late mother and her family. I visited for approximately one week last month. I had not been there since I was a young girl when I left, that was about 55 years ago."

"Well we will have to see about that. According to our records you are a principal in a company doing business with Japan."

"I never was, only an officer. We never had any such formal business with Japan. We only purchased items for our business from them, but not for the last few years when there was a boycott by our country. I am retired and have no relations with the company now. I only have an annuity. My late husband and others founded the company here in the City many years ago. I have no connections and have never been to Japan."

"But madam," the other agent spoke up, "even so, you were recently in Okinawa. And we must further examine you and the business."

Dad explained, "She is from the Ryukyus, in Na'a, Okinawa Island."

The other agent came into the room carrying part of the vellum map from Granma's room. I noticed that it had a large piece missing where it had been torn from the wall.

"This is a Japanese map and has some kind of Japanese writing on it. It could be a secret code," he said.

"That's a map of the Ryukyus with Japan and China. It's where she was born. It used to be an independent kingdom. Japan took it over after she was born," Tomiko said. "We can translate the sayings and names on it if you like."

"It is not code. It is calligraphy in hiragana, script writing. Just shows where she is from. Not code or dakine," I said.

"My, are you a precious little girl," the agent said.

I looked up at him and shook my head and wanted to call him a name back, but was afraid to say anything. He being way so big and Mom would not like me to say those kinds of words, I was thinking.

"Now madam, do you deny that you are a member of Fujidan?"

Granma laughed, "Oh yes, of course, that is the local women's club here in San Francisco," she replied. "It's merely a social club. It's listed in the phone book. That is no secret. My neighbors and friends are members. Many are not even Japanese-Americans."

The agents said that it was necessary for our Grandmother to come with them the following day. That she must bring all the company papers she had and only what personal things she could carry.

"But what has she done? Is she arrested?" We all asked. They didn't answer, just left, saying only that they would return tomorrow.

After the government agents left, everyone talked about them.

"I don't really think they are very friendly or knowledgeable,"Mom said. "That is not good."

The following morning I sat with our Grandmother on the front room couch. "Oh *Sobosan* what am I going to do? I won't sleep if you are gone and we will really miss you and I love you so. You just got to come back real soon, please, Granma. Please."

"Now Kitty, remember this, even if some people are being hateful, just forgive them and just be *Nyokodo*, love your neighbor, no matter what. Remember to *Omoiyari*, keep love in your heart. Now don't forget."

"I promise Granma." That was the last thing she told me when she left.

Before Tomiko came, I sometimes shared the same bedroom with Grandma. I did not like sleeping alone. I went to bed earlier than Tomiko, who had a lot of homework. So it was nice to stay again with Grandma those times.

When I saw the agents' car stop in front of the house I jumped up and left the room. Tomiko answered the door and welcomed the agents in.

While Dad and Tomiko were helping with our Grandmother's luggage, I yelled to them to wait. I was trying to carry an urn almost as big as me. I was in a hurry and screamed. "Stop, please wait, if ya havta take Granma, ya gotta take Granpa too!"

Dad had said that now with the war, we were dealing with "uncertainty". I didn't really know what that meant until I started missing Granma the very next morning after they took her away. We were not told where she was going or when she would return. The family attempted to find information. We received nothing for a long time. It was many months later before we had any news. I think they just did not care.

"Where was she, how long, and was she OK?" Eichi asked the local FBI office in the City. But no one could give him an answer.

He said that when he made his inquiry they asked him many questions, including name, address, social security number, and what school he was attending, which at that time was the local junior college in the City. He said he hoped that the questions would not lead to him being arrested.

"I am afraid that just because I talked to them it might

reflect against me for inquiring about an Issei, our Grandmother. They are so paranoid and have strange ideas about Japanese-Americans. So many just do not seem to differentiate us from Japanese," he said.

I had always liked listening to the radio in the evening. Some of the stories were very exciting and the music was really good. But that was spoiled when we started hearing very frightening things on the radio.

Some organizations were saying that all Japanese-Americans should be deported and that their citizenship be taken away. They said that all of us were spies. There were stories claiming that the Japanese-American islanders aided the Japanese that attacked Pearl Harbor and that the islanders should be tried for treason. I knew that could not have been true. One group was the American Legion. Another was called the Daughters, and Sons of the Golden West, and the Daughters of the American Revolution. They said that they were patriots and we were the enemy. Then we heard that the governor and the state attorney general had agreed that all Japanese-Americans should leave the west coast of the country because we were a threat and in the event of invasion by Japanese armed forces we would be supporting Japanese forces. It was not true and scary and there were so many things said about our parents that were lies and propaganda.

That is when I started to really stay close to Tomiko when we went to and from school. I was so proud of her because she is so much bigger and smarter than lots of kids I feared.

One day, Mom and Granma (before she was arrested)

came home from a PTA meeting with disturbing news. Some people came to the meeting and insisted that Tomiko and me be transferred to another school, in *Nihonmachi*. Called "Japan Town" by some white persons in the City. It was far from our home. We would have had to take some busses. But my parents refused. Granma was very mad when one lady told her that us kids should be in a school only "with your kind".

"What does that mean, 'your kind?' I don't understand," I asked.

"It is nothing, just prejudice and ignorance," Granma said.

What was very sad was that those persons did not want either Tomiko or me ever again to give the Pledge of Allegiance to the classes. We were never asked again. But I still spoke it in class with the others. I was very proud to recite it. Each time I saw the flag in the class and also flying outside it makes me feel so very happy and I would get "chicken skin" (goose bumps) because I am an American citizen and love America. I wish Granma could have been a citizen. It was wrong they did not allow her, or her Issei friends.

In early February of 1942 I started the second grade. I was very happy because Miss Gregory was still my teacher. Things were kind of better. The other kids stopped making faces and calling me names because Tomiko would come to my rescue. But I knew things would still be scary and Tomiko was always with me when we walked home. I still had some good friends whom I was happy to see.

Because of the war, we had to stay home most of the time

with lights out and the windows covered with black shades. We could not travel very far, but Dad and Mom worked close by, so they were still allowed to go to work. Our family had some restrictions, which I did not understand, but I heard all the talk about them.

"Why are we restricted? Obviously they don't trust us. I think it will be soon that we lose some really important freedoms," Eichi said. He had to have special permission to continue his college studies because he had to go to the library in Berkeley.

Eichi was my oldest brother. I always looked up to him. He was smart and also very big. Bigger than Dad and most guys I knew. He would kid me because I am so small for my age, but I knew that he loved me and he was not being harmful. When he heard about the bombing of Pearl Harbor he went with his friends to enlist in the army. They accepted some, but not Eichi or another close friend (an African-American), saying that they were unfit because of their ancestry and race. He was only seventeen years old so he could not have been able to join anyway. Dad wanted him to finish college, and would not have given him permission.

I still did not understand why some people thought that those persons with Japanese ancestry would be disloyal to America. They were citizens and never did anything disloyal like they were being accused. When I asked why, Dad explained about prejudice, ignorance and hate. All of that made me so sad and afraid because there was nothing I could do. Many of the people saying bad things about us on the radio and in newspapers were people in the government. Granma and my parents said we would have to look to President Roosevelt himself for protection, and that he should explain to everyone that we are not the enemy, but are patriotic loyal American citizens.

Then the strangest thing happened in February. Dad, a member of the Japanese American Citizens League (JACL), said that the JACL along with other organizations had officially proclaimed the loyalty of the Nissei community to the United States. Dad said that the JACL had urged its members to give their loyalty to America in early January or late December.

"I am not sure why that was done. They already had proclaimed that we were loyal citizens of America. There is something here I don't understand or like," he said.

A week later, Eichi told everyone there was some very bad news.

DAY OF REMEMBRANCE

On the 19th of February, the president signed an executive order (#9066) that allowed the military to exclude all Japanese-Americans from sensitive areas of the country without trial or hearings because of our Japanese ancestry. Every American citizen, Nisei, and their elders, Issei, who reside on the West Coast.

"Meaning that all of us, even though we are American citizens are going to be incarcerated because we are here on the West Coast and because of our ancestry," Dad said.

"Didn't the president understand how we all feel about our loyalty to the U.S.?" Mom wondered.

"The JACL has urged everyone to cooperate with the government. I have my doubts, but surely they know what the president was doing and what is best for everyone, even if we might have many questions, doubts and things are now so uncertain. It's a time of war and everyone must sacrifice," Dad said. "I will discuss these matters with them when we meet. I still have many questions, including the fact that we are denied due process. The order was illegal."

"No Dad, that is not right. Our citizenship is now in jeopardy. Doesn't that mean we lose our civil rights? I mean, if the presidential order says we must be removed from the West Coast, wouldn't there have to be some due some process to remove everybody affected?" Eichi asked.

A week later, Dad gave us more information after talking to the JACL and also with the American Civil Liberties Union (ACLU).

"We are at war and according to the JACL we all have to sacrifice something and that is why there is a call to cooperate with the government. Remember, it is a presidential order directed at the military authorities. I have also learned that although the order affects our citizenship, the American Civil Liberties Union had agreed with the president's order. Only the San Francisco ACLU chapter had disagreed with their approval. It is apparently powerless to protest, but may still sue for the denial of our civil rights. It would, I understand, be a long time to get the U.S Supreme Court to decide," Dad said.

I just did not understand all what, Dad and Eichi and Michio were saying. They were smarter than me and I couldn't really see or know about everything they said. The news said that the presidential order meant that Japanese-Americans are the ones who are a threat to America and must be removed. That was us. That much I understood.

Yet why should the government see all of us as a threat to America? That is just like all those who don't like us because of our Japanese ancestry. Why do we have to suffer because our ancestry has some Japanese in it? We didn't bomb Hawai'i.

I talked again to my teacher and thought about what was said about all of us going away. I told everyone one night, "I still don't understand. We are just not different. We're Americans just like the ones who don't like us. How can they see us as Japanese when we are not Japanese. We are American citizens like them. Besides, don't they know we don't like the Japanese? They attacked Hawai'i. All of us are at war with that country. Why are we seen differently, now even by our own government?"

Michio reported that his class had attended a congressional hearing and testimony in downtown San Francisco.

"It was very strange and scary. People testified that we are a threat, and must be deported and never come back. Some said mean things about us. And no one testified on our behalf. They said we had no right to speak because we are "Japs." Some in the audience asked why my teacher brought us students to the hearing. Saying that we were not welcome, and that our teacher had no right to bring us, and that we don't have any rights because we are Japs."

"They see us not as Americans but only as Japanese despite of who we really are." Dad said.

"They are ignorant, harboring a lot of envy because we have been successful in spite of their attempting to hinder us, and are jealous, simply disliking us," Mom replied.

"Your Grandmother really had a lot to say about them, recalling how she was treated in Hawai'i and later here. One excuse used for over-throwing the Hawaiian monarchy and annexing the Islands was the so-called fear of the "yellow peril," referring to the immigration of Japanese-Americans and other Asians to the Islands. They also claimed that the Hawaiians were in league with Japan to annex the Islands to that country. All lies and fantasies.

They are the same people still talking about us." Mom concluded.

In the beginning of April, instruction notices were put up around the City for all persons of Japanese ancestry about the evacuation. It was from the Western Defense Command and the Fourth Army. It directed our removal from the first section of the restricted area of the Western United States. Dad said it was from the proclamation of the army general in charge of our western district.

"Dad, we havta leave our homes, everything? But where do we go?" I asked.

"We will be notified very soon. Now we have to start making preparations. We are being told to only pack what we can carry. Soon we have to leave San Francisco. We'll bring only the most important things for travel. All else we will have to store or sell or give away."

"I wish we could go back to Hilo, no one hates us in Hawai'i," Michio said.

"It is a war zone now. The day after Pearl Harbor, the Islands were put under martial law. Like Grandmother, other Issei have been arrested and interned. Our great uncle and other relatives," Eichi said.

"But no Nissei are being evacuated over there, only here. That does not make any sense," Tomiko remarked.
"That is because the general over here hates us. He said we have to leave because we are a threat. He said in the news that a Jap is a Jap, making no exceptions, even if we are citizens and have never broken any laws," Dad said.

"He is the guy who ordered the evacuation, claiming it was due to military necessity and imminent danger," Eichi added. "He admits that there is no proof that we are a security risk. He also said that because there have been no reports of sabotage by the Japanese-American community, proves that those Japs are a danger and threat and must be incarcerated," Eichi quoted him.

By that late March we knew we were to be evacuated.

"There is not much time to get ready to be evacuated from our homes," Mom said. "It's not fair, people are taking advantage us. They offer very little for our property, knowing we are desperate."

When Tomiko and I came home from school, Dad was there and Mom was crying and arguing with, Michio, Eichi and Dad. He was passing out some tags.

"But Dad, they all have the same number, why?" Michio said.

"Michio is right, but there should be all our names," Eichi said.

"Yes, why the single number? You said it is for the whole family, we are not some damn number," Mom said.

"Please let me explain again," Dad interrupted. "It is not my decision or my choice. The authorities told the JACL, who are assisting them, that each family has to be registered prior to being interned, and that the number is a way to keep track of all of us. The JACL had no choice in this, it's the authorities order," Dad said.

He further said, "I am told that the agency running the internment is called the War Relocation Authority (WRA). I had to register all of our names, except Grandmother's, with them, since we have no information on where she is. I have tags for each of us, and they must be kept safe. They show our family number. Please don't lose them or throw them away. It is our identity and the WRA can make trouble if we cannot show them as part of our identification."

LAST DAY HOME

That last day, I could not forget. It was the last day we were packing to move out of our home. It was hard to decide what to leave and what to take. We were sad. All our happiness was gone. I cried a lot, and remember Mom could not talk much, hiding herself, not wanting anyone to see her crying.

That last night I talked to Tomiko, "Grandma and Grandpa helped us so much so we could all be in our own home. We were helping to pay for it, "So now all you children can grow up together," they told us that same first day we all were together after our parents, you, Michio, me and Eichi, arrived from Hilo, and began living all together in our new home. Then, just because of our ancestry we gotta go away. Just all of a sudden go away. And not go away mad, but go away! Now where are we going to live?"

"Kitty, all I know is that the WRA and the army are putting everyone in some sort of big assembly areas while camps are now being built for all of us."

I told her that I was not going to wear any number tag. It was just not me. I didn't care what some people said. I am still me, Miyako, not a part of some damn number. I said that I was not going away anywhere. I was going to stay home. Our home. "Where we are now."

"Oh Kitty, quiet down. Mom and Dad won't like you talking like that," Tomiko said.

That last night, I talked to Grandma in my heart. She had taught me to do that when there was some loved one who was not there and I was alone.

"Dear *Sobosan*, we love you. How are you? We have to go away too. I hope we will learn where you are and that you can learn where we are too. You may get a number. We have one for the whole family. Sorry, but we could not put you on it. They are tags with a big number for the family, but no name. I not like that. Hope you won't be too mad at me, because I said some really bad things about those tags, but I don't think you will like them, or you might already have to wear one?"

After I said goodbye to Grandma I still could not sleep. Soon we were going to be like her. We didn't know where she was and maybe no one would know where we would be. We could be lost somewhere and no one would even care, never ever.

"Kitty, what is the matter?" Tomiko was holding me. "Are you OK? You have been screaming and crying. Mom even heard you."

"Oh, I was scared, I'm sorry, just afraid. Not mean to wake anyone."

Tomiko talked to me and hugged me, everything seemed so bad and scary, I must have been crying awful loud. Next thing it was morning. I still didn't feel very good. Everyone was awake and Mom told us we have to hurry downtown. We had a ride to where everyone was meeting with our travel bags and other stuff we had to carry. Then she told us the good news.

"We just received a letter from our Grandmother. She is in Texas at a women's internment camp. There is no address, but we can reply to the WRA. Someone has blacked out some of the letter. It says that she is doing fine now, but she has been sick and had to wait a long time to see a doctor. She sends us her love and asks us not to worry. She says she knows several of the women there, but is warned not to say anything about who they are or where they are from."

"She won't be back will she? She is lost just like we will be." I cried.

"Oh no Kitty, we don't know that, you have to be brave. Remember what she told us, have *gaman*, persevere and keep going," Mom said.

When we arrived downtown it was chilly and overcast. Another unhappy day, Tomiko, Michio and me ended up sitting with our stuff. Eichi, Mom and Dad were nearby talking to other grownups. There was a big soldier near. I went over to him.

"Hi, my name is Miyako, but you can call me Kitty, thank you for guarding our stuff." He kind of smiled, but did not say anything. I think he was shy. Another family was next to us, they smiled and I think laughed a little. I didn't understand why, he seemed nice. Then some big busses came and soldiers ordered each family to board.

That is when I asked a soldier: "What about our things? Do we put them on the buses with us, some are really big?"

"No, no, you go, get on the bus, don't you understand little girl?" He spoke very harshly and I ran quickly to the bus.

"Gee, he didn't have to yell like that," someone said.

I had never been on such a big bus. It had really nice big soft seats for two persons. I had to climb a little to get into mine. Our school busses were smaller and had only smooth wooden seats that fit lots of us kids at once. Then, all of a sudden we started moving. I think we were going south through the City, but the window shades were closed. Someone said that the soldiers wanted the shades shut, but since I was sitting next to the window I was able to peek out a little. No one seemed to mind and the soldiers did not see me. We were going south from the City on the Junipero Serra highway. I knew because we studied about that. Then I was not sure where we were after that.

It was Monday and I should have been in school, not on some bus. I really missed school already. Just last Friday was the last day of school for Tomiko and me, but it was wrong because there was more school left for us to complete. We would miss the last month and more. That was not fair. Somebody did not care about us students, just in a hurry to get us out of our homes.

There was only a little while before the school semester finished. And I hoped that whoever rented our home would take care of it, our little garden too. I would miss so many things. I hoped I might find out who would rent our home, get their name and write them. Miss Gregory had given me the addresses of my school friends I could write. I wanted to practice writing. It was going to be lonely wherever we went.

TANFORAN

Someone said, "We are here, it's the race track."

"What? What is that?" I asked.

"This is Tanforan, where they race horses, but now you will be staying here," the bus driver said.

Gee, I thought, Horses, I can get to see horses again. I missed them from our visits to the zoo and the ones the police rode on in the Park. Horses were so beautiful and big, and seemed so friendly. Maybe I could get to ride one and talk to it like I had heard and seen in movies and heard about on the radio.

After the bus stopped inside Tanforan we were all registered. We all had to show the family tag, mine too. When we finished we had to wait for our luggage. I asked if I could look for the horses. Dad said it was okay. He told me where to meet and not to take too long or get lost.

It was a big place. I watched other buses as they let people off, so many, hundreds or even thousands of people I guessed. Eichi had said that all were mostly from San Francisco, the Peninsula, and the Oakland Bay area.

I didn't know where to start looking for horses. I just walked and looked. There were a lot of buildings with signs saying, "stables," but no horses, only some workers building and painting. In the middle of the park there was a huge grandstand with some of the people sitting on the bleachers. I asked. They had not seen any horses. Some more workers were building below the grandstand and said they had never seen any horses and that they had been there for a week.

I followed the fence where we first came into the park. A long time later, I was back where our bus went through a gate into the park. It was locked. I got confused. All the time I asked about the horses, still, nobody knew. I got hungry. I had not had much breakfast because I was not feeling good about leaving home. A nice group of people had given us lunches, some sandwiches, apples and veggies. I stopped near a pond and ate some.

I was getting tired so I just watched all the people. It was hard to believe there were so many and that they were all Japanese ancestry, now so many in the racetrack. I knew they also could not stay in their home anymore. I felt sad. I just wanted to go home really soon, maybe right then. I still didn't understand why some people, the government and even important people like governors and congressmen wanted us to leave. It was hard to believe they were prejudice like Eichi and Dad said.

I could see lots of people and none looked anything like the pictures the newspapers had of Japanese soldiers. Those pictures also had strange cartoon kind of drawings labeled as Japanese. Michio said that the newspaper and magazine people made ordinary persons look like ugly comics so people would hate Japanese and think that all Japanese looked like that. Why would they mix us up with the Japanese who were fighting America in the War? Japan was thousands of miles away, twice as far as Hawai'i. I just did not understand.

It seemed to be getting late, so I looked for where Dad had said the family would be, but I was not sure, nothing looked the same as I remembered. There were many families making mattresses with the piles of straw that had been dumped near the stables and the barracks. All were very friendly, but did not know where my family was nor had seen any horses.

I looked some more where other families were unpacking their belongings. The sun was setting. There were big shadows that I think were from the San Mateo Mountains.

I saw some soldiers near one of the gates. I called to them, but they ignored me. I yelled and shook the gate fence until one saw me and walked over.

"Pardon me, Mr. Soldier, my name is Miyako. You can call me Kitty. Can you tell me where the horses are please? I can't find them."

He looked at me and said, "You, little girl, stay back from the fence. Where are your parents? Now git, go on, git!"

I didn't know that word. He had some kind of an accent. And he didn't tell me about the horses. I waited and banged again on the fence and yelled about the horses.

He came back, very angry, "Hey, I said git! Git! Ya damn little Jap brat!"

"Please Mr. Soldier, I am sorry, I just want to see some

horses," I said. Then he suddenly picked up a rifle and pointed it at me,

"Now git!" he yelled again.

I ran and screamed. I could hear him and other soldiers laughing. He didn't shoot me, but I was so scared I did not stop running until I was between some buildings, not even looking back. I got out of breath and cried.

It was dark then and I was lost. I had lost my family and was really in trouble and could not see. I did not know where I was. It started to rain a little. When I had been running I had fallen and dropped my sack lunch. I managed to find it, but my apple had rolled out. I could hear it but not find it. Then I bumped into a porch. I felt a door that was locked, I knocked and yelled but no one was there. I was crying and very scared. There was no one around and I was lonely. I knew I had not paid attention to the time and was in trouble. I used my blouse to wipe my tears. I didn't know what to do. I leaned against the door and squeezed myself close because it was getting cold and I was really tired, cold, shivering and sleepy.

"Kitty, wakeup. You have to get up and come. We don't have much time," Tomiko was shaking me.

"Oh, where am I? I got lost and have plenty trouble."

"You are in our room, you been sleeping. We found you last night. You were sleeping by one of the barracks."
"I'm going to be punished now, aren't I?"

"No, I don't think so. We were really worried and just

happy you were found safe."

"Something is pilau (Hawaiian for "stink"), what is it?" I asked.

"Oh, it's our rooms, we are in a part of one of the stables. That smell is from the horses, but it is where we have to live now. We might get an apartment later, " Tomiko said.

"But where are the horses? All day I looked for them, they are not in Tanforan now, just us. We can't stay in here. We are not horses. We should just go home. OK? Please, wouldn't it be all right? Let's go right now," I asked.

"No Kitty, we can talk later. Now we must not be late for breakfast. Hurry. There is no time to waste. Then after that we have to get examined."

I followed her as best I could. I was still tired from yesterday. We came to a big building where there were some people waiting in lines. Tomiko handed me a spoon and plate. It was a crowded place with many tables and people in lines to get their food like the cafeterias at school, but big lines. It was a noisy place, everyone talking at once.

"This place is called a "mess" by the army guys," Tomiko said. "I don't like it, but it is where we have got to eat."

I didn't like it either and did not want to eat there, but I was hungry. I could not see the rest of the family. I found out later that because of the crowds that people didn't always eat together like a family. That made Mom very unhappy. "We must always stay together as a family,"

Mom had insisted. After we ate the strange army food, Tomiko grabbed my hand,

"Come, come, now we have to be examined by doctors," she said. I followed her and found more long lines near the grandstand. That was where the little hospital was being put together.

It took most of the morning and I was so tired that I just squatted every once in a while. When we got inside one of the buildings we had to undress and put on some white robes. The nurses poked us really funny. I was embarrassed because one doctor would look so strange at me, I didn't like him. I closed my eyes, did not want to look. And did not like it when he treated me like a little girl and patted me on the head and said I was very healthy. I already knew that I was healthy, so I didn't have to get examined and be so embarrassed. I could not help crying a little when they stuck me, vaccinations are real hurt. I tried hard not to cry, being kind of little, I didn't want anyone to think I was being a baby. After that, I found Mom and Dad.

"Oh Kitty, we were very worried last night. We are so happy we found you," Mom hugged me.

"I'm sorry I got lost, everything is so big and crowded and confusing. Now I got really sore arms," I complained.

"Oh dear, I am sorry, we had your medical cards, but I don't think anyone told us about those exams. We don't blame you, all this is such chaos, we are just glad we are now together."

"Thanks for finding me Mom, Dad, Eichi, Michio and Tomiko. I'm still tired. Is it OK if I go and rest?" I asked.

I slept until they called me to dinner. Our pilau place, stable, was almost nothing but stuffed lumpy mattresses on top of squeaky iron cots, and our bags and luggage.

You almost could not move between the beds. I still like horses, but I know I would never get used to the smell and the dust and dirt. It sometimes made me sneeze. At dinner we managed to sit together in the mess. Mom was happy because it worried her when we did not eat together. It was hard for Mom, she missed our normal mealtime it was her special time. The food the army gave us was bad. I do not understand how the army people can eat some stuff they call food. It was hard not being able to get used to that stuff. To just remember it makes me ill. I was sick from it many times and had to wash out private things sometimes.

Living in that racetrack was hard on everybody. Often there was no water and when there was, it was always cold, even for showers. Of course, there was no privacy with any personal stalls and you were never alone to do very personal things.

Why were we treated like that? Finally more lights were installed to make it easier to visit the restrooms at night. I wondered if the army people who ran the place lived like that.

Every night I tried to go to sleep. I always wanted to go home. Some of the kids I saw said it was like a great big camp. Not me, it was like Mom called it, "chaos," a new word for me.

It was always noisy. Not just nights but days. Different than the noise I remembered that last day in the home, in an empty house and the echo I made each time I stomped my feet. What we didn't give away we had to store under the house. And there we were with nothing but reminders of where we were happy.

My teacher and some of the school kids in my class had quietly given me a little party and a card with nice messages. I had hid it in my suitcase, but I didn't want to see it for a long time. I didn't want a party or anything else, just to go home.

That day was sad for Tomiko too. We were walking down the school hall for the last time when she grabbed my hand, "come, let's go fast", making me run to keep up with her. She was crying, she had seen a boy she liked who no longer would talk to her after Pearl Harbor.
I still liked and missed that school, even if so many did not like us anymore. There were good teachers and still a few kids who were my friends.

We heard we might be able to move out of the horse stables when more barracks were finished. Dad, Eichi and even Michio were able to get little jobs to help with construction and work on more restrooms and other facilities. But they said that the wages were really low.

"Only a fraction of what they should have given us," Dad complained.

We all missed Granma and hoped she would get over being sick. It was not fair that she was not able to see a doctor. She was taking care of all our monies and savings, but the government, we found out, had frozen it because she was suspected of things I didn't understand.

Because of the noise, I also missed the music Granma had. She would play records on the gramophone. We would dance and sing. Everyone clapped to it. Now there was just talking everywhere and I wanted to close myself so I could not hear. That made me wonder many times what was really wrong with us that all we could do was now only remember. I still just wanted to go home. Nothing was supposed to be like this ever.

Tanforan had a store that sold what Mom called supplemental items that the family did not bring. Over counter medicines like cough drops, aspirin, hand and laundry soaps and other foods that the mess did not provide. Unfortunately the supplies were always low or sold out.

"We must be very careful of anything we spend. That means that we should not buy anything outside of the meals we get," Mom said.

I went with her and found a store set up where other foods, and magazines and newspapers were sold, but it was very small and did not have much to sell. Most of the time when we looked for something we needed it had been sold out. Things like aspirin, tooth paste or toenail clippers, little things we most needed were hard to find.

It was hard enough staying in that pilau, (stinky), stable, but the worst part was that there weren't enough bathrooms and no privacy. For instance, toilet stalls without doors. It was really embarrassing. I could not really talk about it. But the stables did not smell as bad when the sewers started smelling. They had not been finished or had broken down. I asked a couple times how long we had to be in Tanforan the way it was. There was no answer and I was tired of asking. I just wanted to go home.

Mom managed to find some work in the mess and also within the schools that were setup that summer. She started getting a little happier. Michio found some other boys to hang out with. He also enjoyed some of the classes and playing ball. So with the rest of the family occupied, only Tomiko and I were mostly alone. She found some books to read that university people had donated. I just wanted to be by myself. Just think about our home. Nothing else. I found a nice cozy place on the stadium steps to sit and watch most of the camp.

I started thinking about our garden that I helped Grandpa make. It made me happy remembering the different colored flowers, the winding rock path with white pebbles, soft green grasses, the sky, so blue with funny clouds. I was lying there and wanted to stay forever when I herd some giggles and laughing. I looked up to see some kids running by the stadium chasing each other. I was sad, the garden was gone, but I felt better having remembered.

Leaving the steps, I found my way under the grandstand where there were hundreds of men camped. There were rows of boxes, bags and luggage. They were busy talking, visiting, meeting and some were playing board games. One man who reminded me of my Grandfather looked up and gave me a big friendly smile,

"Oh hi-o, how are you young lady? What is your name, may I ask?" he gave a little bow.

"Miyako, but you can call me Kitty, everyone does," I answered.

"Well, what do you think of where we are? All of us away from home and in this strange war and times."

"I want to go home. Don't belong here, maybe nobody does. And not really know why we are locked up. Didn't do anything wrong," I answered him, and started to cry a little, but tried to hide it so he not think I was acting like a baby.

"That, Kitty is very good. I see you are a young lady who understands some things and also knows and admits that there is so much we do not understand. My name is H. Omori."

We talked and he asked me about my family and told me all about living by himself in the City. He worked for the state until he was fired for his ancestry. He was sitting at a small table with other men who had also been fired in the same way. He introduced me to his friends and showed me a couple of games they had been playing, Go and Shiigo. I did not understand them.

One man invited me to sit and play his turn. Of course I did not really play. He would whisper each move in his language. I did not really understand his Japanese, but we won. It was fun, even if I was not sure what I was doing. I felt embarrassed when they congratulated me and said I did OK and should return sometime. I had a new good friend, Mr. Omori and the other gentlemen.

One day I heard someone in the stables playing music.
They had brought an electric phonograph. The family also
had a little portable radio. Only a very few had radios. Dad
said we were only supposed to bring what we could carry
and we still had not managed to bring everything that was
essential.

Michio complained because he lost his shortwave radio to
the FBI. They did not inform us that regular radios were
acceptable. We all missed the radio programs and the
music. Once in a while I was able to hear a radio playing
in a stable near ours. It was nice, but often made me
homesick.

When we finally got the rest of our luggage, I found the
little suitcase I got when I came from Hilo. I looked and
looked through the case, but could not find something I
had packed that was special to me. It was not there. Then
mom asked me if she could help.
"No, that's OK, but I think I might have put some things in
one of the big clothes bags."

She found a couple of bags and let me look, but I could not
find it. I didn't want to say what I was looking for,
because was afraid Michio would kid me about it. As long
as I remember I had a little panda. It was the one special
pal I had and sometimes just wanted it near me. But now
being six years old I did not want anyone to think I was
being a baby.

Once a long time ago someone asked me what I called my
panda.

"I named him Panda," I said.

They laughed and said that's not a name. I kept him hidden after that. Dakine was private and personal.

I looked very hard for a long time. But I could not find it, I lost it and that was another sadness to go with all the other sadness things.

About a month after we arrived, Tomiko and I went to the post office next to one of the gates to receive the family's mail. It was very crowded and we had a long wait. She gave the guard Dad's authorization paper and we were given a stack of mail.

"Look Kitty, one big envelope is addressed to you and me."

As soon as we got back to the stables we opened it. There were letters from my teacher, Miss Gregory, and also from Tomiko's teacher. Also certificates for both of us. They said we had completed the whole semester, even though we had to leave early. The letter from my teacher thanked me for my studies, listed my grades, and stated that everyone was sorry we had to be evacuated. There were some notes from special classmates with addresses asking me to write and tell them about everything I was doing. Tomiko also got notes from her classmates.

I was so excited that I took everything of mine to show Mr. Omori and his friends. He congratulated me and told me to not stop going to school anywhere we may go.

"I hear that there will soon be some regular schools here at

Tanforan, best you not miss them," he said, thanking me for showing him my certificate and school grades.

I never met so many different people in one place. So many kids I don't know. Then I started to remember some kids all the way back to Hilo and the kids in our neighborhood in San Francisco, besides those in school. I felt kinda lonely. Tomiko understood and said I should now try to make some new friends.

It was hard though and when I had some trouble and did not know what to do, I would run to Tomiko, "What do I do? The kids I wanted to talk to confuse me. They are speaking Japanese, but I don't know how to say anything. I am embarrassed and, you know, I'm shy. I'm afraid. What do I do? How come they talk Japanese?"

"They learned it from some of their parents. Some even were sent to learn after regular school because their family wanted them to speak the language of their heritage. Do you remember some of the kids in Hawai'i had learned Hawaiian or Filipino? And remember, you got your pidgin in the neighborhood where we lived," Tomiko explained.

"Is that why we never learned much Japanese?" I asked.

"Well, we have been Americanized and in Hawai'i it was just simply different. I don't think our parents wanted us to learn lots of Japanese since we were so many generations removed," she answered. "Besides, it might have been different if we had lived near a *Nihonmachi* (Japanese) school like some of them in Hilo."

I felt better and understood that some kids might be

speaking Japanese. I still had trouble making new friends because I didn't know where to begin and because I was always so shy, and upset with everything. I just wanted to go home. And I still carried my bigger problem of why was I supposed to be different from other kids?

In San Francisco, we were all Americans but they started calling Tomiko and me "Jap." It just never would make sense that I could be both Japanese and American at the same time. I not remember ever being called Japanese-American, until after Pearl Harbor got bombed. And then suddenly there were people who blamed us because of our ancestry. Stupidly believing we are the same people as the Japanese thousands of miles away on the other side of the Pacific Ocean.

I remembered that day at school when Tomiko said we looked different, but I just couldn't see that. I thought she had to be mistaken. Mom said that I have to like myself just like I am so I can like everyone else. How can somebody not like us, or do they not like themselves? It was all so strange.

On the school grounds one day at lunch I had asked Tomiko, "How can we be different? We are the same. I never learned any of what you are telling me or how we can be different."

"Kitty, just look around. You and I don't look like the kids here at school."

"Well, that is because we are sisters, you and me."

"No, no, that is not what I mean. Oh never mind for now,

you gotta figure it out for yourself."

"Why? Why do I gotta figure it out when I don't know how to do that?"

Since then, I kept asking myself that question. I still don't know how to figure all that out. It makes me mad, and sometimes I feel like crying about that stuff. All I wanted to do was just be me. When Tomiko did not seem to help me, I tried thinking about all the people I saw. I walked along the path next to the fence that went around the whole Tanforan camp like one big circle. It was funny because I could hear them also talking to themselves. I thought that maybe they had problems too and were trying to figure out their problems.

The fence and gates around the camp had barbed wire and more and more soldiers. I knew now they were not there for protecting us like someone said, but for keeping us in. Eichi had said that kids like me were a danger to other people, so we were evacuated. I knew he was sort of kidding, but that he was really serious too.

I wondered, "What if we never ever could go back out of the gate we came through?" I remembered watching the last families come to Tanforan.

As the soldiers closed the gates behind and locked all of us in, I was mad, really mad. Would any of us ever go back through that gate? Are us little kids really a danger? Did that mean from then on we were supposed to grow up and live differently? That when those gates closed, our lives were gone, and we were no more, gone forever?

I walked to the stables. Mom was sorting some clothes and I hugged her. "Kitty, how nice, but why are you crying?"

I just shook my head and laid down on a bed, I didn't answer her. I couldn't, I did not know what to say. She smiled, hugged me and went back to her work. I went to sleep. When I awoke she was gone.

I took Mr. Omori's advice and went looking for the schools that were being started. I did not want to look for classes in my grade because I felt so bad about missing the days they took from us. Then I discovered that some books were being donated for a library. For some days I looked at the ones I could read. Sometimes it was hard because there were only textbooks that were for high school grades, but nothing I found of interest, except a little dictionary. Later, I did find some books I liked, stories and one reference book of science. I was able to take them out. Much later, when I wanted a book they did not have, I asked the librarian and one of the teachers about going to the library in San Bruno. They said I had to go to a camp administrator. I wrote a neat message to him and later returned when he was in his office.

"So you are the little one who wrote me. My answer is of course. no. Now just run along. I'm very busy."

I wanted to yell at him that I was not a little one but a grown up girl. When he said it, he had patted me on the head like some little doggie. I had taken a lot of time to write him and then wait to see him and he really told me nothing. I was really hurt.

Tomiko was able to take a cooking class taught by a

college student who had experience. "I'm lucky, I'm learning about a lot of gourmet cooking and some special European and Asian cooking," she said.

Mom had a part-time job in the mess, but did not like it because there was no variety of dishes. "Those army and other government guys do not have any good choices and they don't believe that women should be chefs. They are strange," she concluded.

I finally found where some of the horses were. Just across from the camp. In a field, but no stable. We were living in their home. That made me mad. Don't they know the difference between animals and people? Later I also learned that the stables made some people sick breathing that stuffy air and were infected from the unclean dust of the horses in the stables. At least the horses were in the open where the air was better.

We kept our outside doors open because of the bad dust and stink air and had to keep cleaning all the time. Some people put up rows of sticks and cardboard they called barriers to stop the wind off the Bay from blowing cold air into the stables and barracks during the evening and night. It really worked well, but everyone had to take the barriers of sticks and cardboard down because the administration said it did not look good. Some barriers kept going up. People were getting colds. It was things like that and other things that did not make sense.

I was glad that my friends at home did not see me since it was so hard in Tanforan to keep as clean and tidy as Granma and Mom wanted me when I went to school or played in the neighborhood. Sometimes I laughed at what I saw when I looked in the restroom mirror. We did not ever have enough soap for anything. Only little bars we brought, and they were quickly worn out. One neighbor called the camp, "a useless place."

The most uncertain place, I thought, was the mess. Some kinds of food, like canned meat made me sick. I vowed to never eat them again! I did not like having to secretly wash out my private clothes when that stuff made me sick. Once I tried to hang something to dry in the wash area. It was stolen. Maybe someone just could not afford their own things. The food got a little better, but still never like we had at home. Mom still would get upset when we couldn't eat together. Sometimes it was too crowded and kids like me forgot and would eat with other kids instead of with the family. Then like others, I would eat what I could stand and then sneak back in another line and get something better until I was no longer hungry, which was often.

I finally met more friends after I started going to the library. One was Yuke (that means "snow"), she was from Oakland. And there was Rika, from San Jose, plus some others whose names I forgot. Rika was about my age, but even smaller than me, just as shy and also had a little voice. We really got along well and sometimes read a book out loud for practice like our teachers wanted. She didn't know Japanese either so was glad when I told her I hoped that we could learn a little. But we could not find a class. There was one teacher we met who did give us some lessons and papers with what she called conversation words we could practice with and learn.

I still could not understand why our ancestry was different. I asked Yuke one day: "Why are we so different? I mean, does everyone here really look like their Japanese ancestors?"

Yuke looked at me kind of funny, "Well, yeah, we are, don't you know that? Can't you see that?"

I looked at her and said, "No, I don't know, I don't understand and don't know what to see, what to look for. We are all Americans, but I just don't understand why we have to be locked up. How are we different?"

She looked at me, shook her head and left. I felt bad and confused. Did I ask the right question? I knew that maybe I might never figure it out. I was sad and cried right there where I stood. I didn't care if any one saw me.

Mr. Omori listened to my problem. He didn't treat me strangely or laugh at me. He seemed to understand how I just could not figure out why I could not see any differences.

"Well Kitty, maybe you don't really have a problem. What you tell me is not as important or as serious as you think. There is nothing for you to work out or figure out. Not from what you tell me. Nor is there really anything wrong in the questions you raise. It is what we say, '*shi kata ganai.*'

"Oh I have heard my Dad and Grandma say that, but not sure what it means. I know that it is a Japanese saying that is important. Can you explain what it means and how can that help me."

"It simply means that you cannot do anything about it."

"But then what do I do? Or maybe not do? I still don't understand."

He smiled, "I'm sorry if I confuse you. First we are all here together. Locked up because of some peoples' bias and the hysteria of war. They used their influence to force their meaningless views upon our shortsighted government that locked us up and we cannot do anything about it – *shi kata ganai.*

Second, Kitty, your difficulty in figuring it out is really not necessary. You have a gift. So don't worry. Just keep seeing with your heart, and not with your eyes."

"Then that is why I cannot do anything about it?"

"Yes, because there is nothing you need to figure out," he said.

I thanked him and told him how I loved him, and how much he reminded me of my Grandpa.

Then I heard the news that someday all of us in Tanforan would have to leave for one of the new internment camps. Eichi said that one of his college professors told him that the camps were not really internment camps, but concentration camps.

"That was because none of us were given any kind of due process before being interned," said Eichi. "Not a single one of us was afforded the constitutional right to a hearing or other process to determine whether we should be interned, locked up," he explained. "Some would call it judgment without trial."

Later, in the middle of August, Dad found out that most of us would be going to Utah. The WRA would be opening a total of ten camps. One of them would be Topaz, named after mountains in southeastern Utah. I tried to look it up in the library, but could only find information about the mountain range.

I asked a teacher. She said that the camp seems to be in a mainly desert area. Located above sea level by many thousands of feet. "That means it will be very cold in winter and very hot in summer. I have to surmise that it is somewhere south east of Salt Lake," she said.

The family talked over what the teacher said about the cold in Utah. Eichi and Dad were able to get more warm blankets and we got some of our clothes that were in storage. Our former San Francisco neighbor, the Desparis', helped us. They were allowed to meet us at the gate, but not allowed to visit inside Tanforan. We had a limited time to visit them through the locked fence. It was still good to see them, even for that short time. We waved goodbye, not knowing when we would ever see them again.

TRAIN TO CAMP

We watched in late August as the first groups boarded trains. Our train, was a few weeks later. The fences and gates were folded away so the train could be switched to tracks near the racetrack. By the time it was our turn, Tanforan was almost empty of people. Like other trains, ours was very old and had wooden benches for seats.

"It's just like the camp, dirty, dusty and rusty," I said.

There were no sleeping cars, just what Dad called day coaches, and we were really packed. Every seat was taken and I saw that some kids had to sit on their parents' laps.

I stared at the camp, as the train started moving. At first it seemed like the camp was moving and we were standing still. Not wanting to go to Utah, but watching Tanforan slowly disappear made me happy.

The soldiers were all on the train. They had a comfortable coach. During the day they would patrol back and forth through the cars. I guess they thought we were going to jump out or something. They pulled all the shades down. Soon the air became stuffy, humid and very uncomfortable as the day warmed.

"Why can't we open the window shades?" Michio asked.

"They don't want those outside to see us leave," Eichi said. "No one is supposed to know we are going by. We are no longer part of their community."

"You mean we are never coming back. Isn't it our country too? We have also lived here," I said.

I could not help but cry. I kept thinking, we did not have a home anymore. I wondered what Grandpa would have thought. He worked so hard to help us. And Granma, somewhere in Texas, really loved our home. Remembering so much made me so sad. It was too hard not to cry.

As the train gained speed it rocked and swayed. I could hear the wheels go click and clack. After a while it made me sleepy. Each coach had one lantern that hung from the ceiling that swayed back and forth, throwing its light every which ways.

"I can't read with that crazy light, I wish I could turn it off," Michio complained. He gave up and tried to sleep like the rest of us.

After a while I decided to look for a new seat. It's just so crowded and the train makes me so sad. Going away from home and happiness. Maybe I could see another part of the train. I explored all over, still trying to think about our home. I was becoming exhausted. We were going away from our lives and I only wanted to go home. I found a place under a seat. I was very dizzy and tired and it was a cozy place.

Oh, I can see a nice light and some houses and a street. It's ours, and there is our house. It's so quiet but I wonder if I am late or home too early? There's the gate and the garden. The grass is nice and soft and the house is cool.

The chimes are tinkling in the breeze. The sun, the sky, the flowers look nice, oh that is so happy. I will just stay until dinner or maybe later. It is nice to look up and see the clouds and sea gulls from the ocean.

Oh, is it dinner? I can hear Tomiko. She must be calling me home.

"Kitty, Kitty, I'm glad I found you. You missed dinner. Come, come it's this way to the dinner car. We might still be able to get you something. You should not hide like that, we were all so worried."

"What do you mean? What dinner car? Let's just go into the house. No, don't pull me, why are you doing that? That's not the way."

"Kitty, it's the dinner car here on the train. I'll ask the attendant for some food for you," Tomiko said.

"Please sir, this is my little sister, she missed the meal. Can we get something for her, she is very hungry?"

"Well hello, what a lovely girl you are, let me see if I can find something. We cannot have anyone go hungry on this train. Here, it looks like we can get you a nice sandwich and something to drink. What is your name?"

I spoke up, "Well, I'm Kitty, that's what they call me. My name is really Miyako. But what are you doing here? Is this near our home? I don't understand."

The nice gentleman looked at me and then to Tomiko and asked, "What is she talking about?"

"Oh, my sister . . . she is just a little tired and forgot where we are."

"Thanks for the sandwich, maybe my Mom can ask you how to make it, it was very good. Do you want to meet her? Our house is just over there ... oh, I think, it's not far ... eh ... I ... don't know."

Tomiko grabbed my hand. "Thanks Mister, we havta get back."

She hurried me along, then stopped and looked at me. "What are you talking about? Don't you know where we are?"

"We, we are home. I never saw a Negro man live near here before. He is so big and handsome and nice. Did he just move in? He is the nicest man. Hope we get to visit. Maybe see his family, and if he has some kids we could get to know them," I said.

Tomiko looked at me and shook her head and frowned.

"It's getting late, why don't you just sit next to me, there's room. You look tired and confused," She said.

"Oh no I'm not, we can stay up, I been having such a good time. But is there school tomorrow?"

Tomiko didn't answer. She was sleeping when I looked at her. "Good night, I guess I'll stay here for now," I said.

Something woke me. I think the train slowed down. Then I heard someone say that we were going into the mountains.

It seemed to get cooler. Then the train made a jolt, the wheels made a big squeak, we slowed to a stop.

"What is going on?" I asked Tomiko.

"I think we are stopping for something, come, it looks like everyone's going outside."

As we stepped down from the train I suddenly felt warm air rushing to meet us. We had to walk along the train in a narrow line because the soldiers were keeping everyone from wandering far from the train tracks. Someone said we had reached the Nevada desert.

"Never seen a desert before. Sure is hot, you can see forever and ever. Just full of nothing out there," I said. "Gee, no one would want to live in a desert."

Then the train gave one long whistle and we had to get back on board.

When I returned to where Tomiko was sitting she asked me, "Do you feel OK now? I mean, did you get enough sleep last night?"

"Oh yeah," I said. "But I just don't understand where we are going, do we still have to go to Utah? I want to go home still, very, very soon. We need to take care of the house, we cannot stay away."

"You do remember? We left the house way back in San Francisco, now we are somewhere in Nevada."

I tried to say something, but was so sleepy and tired.

Later when I awoke Tomiko was cuddling and holding me close and wiping my face. "You have been crying and crying. But you slept for a long time. Now let's go get something to eat."

I liked eating on the train, the food was really good and I didn't remember my last meal. I was thinking it was just before we got on the train at Tanforan. I felt happy to be away from there. I hoped that I could see my friends again and we would have a nice place to sleep that did not stink.

The train trip seemed to just get harder. Nothing much to do and after a while I was not sure what time or what day it was. I'm glad I didn't remember my dreams because they seemed really bad, like a few times when we first came to Tanforan.

Some dreams were during the day, not just at night. I could not see how anyone could enjoy all the hotness and sweat and rocking and swaying of the train. There were not enough stops and when we did stop I had a hard time standing up. I could not remember how long we were on the train. I was so sad and kept going to sleep, being so tired and worried about our home.

"Tomiko, Tomiko, where you go? We just stopped and everybody is getting off, can't find anybody." Then someone called to me.

"Kitty, isn't that your name? I saw your family looking and calling for you. They just left the train. You will find them by the buses."

The train trip was over. I ran down the train steps yelling,

"Here I am, I'm here, over here." It was very sunny and I could hardly see with the sun in my eyes.

Then I saw Tomiko in front of some buses. "Kitty, over here!"

The ground was very hard and smelled like salt.

"We are in a part of the great Salt Lake," someone said.

But it was all dirty, I thought it would be nice and white, but people had been making it dirty walking on it.

"Where have you been Kitty?" Tomiko asked. "We waited for you. The family left on one of the buses so I've been waiting and hoping to find you. We can catch up when we get to the camp. All the buses are going to the same place. Just hope it's nicer than where we were."

"Still want to go home, just home, that's where we live. Dis bus is like the train, so old and rusty and noisy and bumpy," I said.

"Well, that's no real road we are on, just desert out there and we are going sort of south," Tomiko said.

"Wish we could have gone somewhere in Salt Lake City, lots of nice places there, the teacher at Tanforan showed me on the map."

"Yeah, I can't see anything along here but dirt and desert here an there," I said pointing toward what looked like mountains through the dust. "I remember now what that teacher showed me. I think the new place is near a desert

which will be cold at night because we will be thousands
of feet above sea level,"

Tomiko just shook her head and went to sleep. I was
sitting by the window looking out, watching telephone
poles go by until I got sleepy. But then we started through
a town. I was hoping it would be where we could live.

"Gee," Tomiko said, "look at all the houses and trees, what
town is this?"

"It's called Delta," I answered. "I think we are near some
water. I learned that word from our books at home."

But the buses didn't stop and we soon saw more bare hills
and the desert.

TOPAZ

After about an hour someone cried out, "I think this is the camp."

But all I could see were clouds of dust. It was windy. Then I saw long dark shadows coming out of the dust and other buses in front of us. The shadows were long black buildings with a big fence around them. As we stopped and everyone started leaving I could hear some kind of music being played and barely see a sign that said, "Welcome to Topaz Internment Camp."

"No," I said, shaking my head while trying to keep hold of Tomiko's hand against the wind and dust. It was thick and almost as deep as me. "No, no, dis is da desert, it's not dakine for a home."

Then we saw the rest of the family. They were waiting for us. "Where were you?" Dad asked, "I'm glad you are OK, but I hope it's the last time we have to worry. Please, don't do that anymore." He was angry, but still happy to see me.

"I'm sorry, I had been sleeping and didn't hear anyone. I'm sorry, I won't get lost again," I told Dad.

He had been explaining to the soldier who was holding up the family from entering the camp.

"Oh, is that the child that was lost? She's only a baby. That is not good, next time we will have to make a formal report. Someone might consider that is child neglect," the soldier said.

"No, I'm not a baby, dummy. I'm a grown up girl. I'm six and 8 months of age and not like what you said." I was mad, but Dad was madder.

"Now Kitty, you cannot talk to him that way, tell him you are sorry."

I apologized and the soldier smiled. I could see that Michio and Eichi were smiling to themselves. I hoped they were not laughing at me. I had been insulted, even if I was being rude. Mom was embarrassed. She did not say anything. She didn't like what I said.

While we registered and were being examined by the camp medical staff, I wandered off to talk to some of the people working in the camp.

"Hi, my name is Miyako, but you can call me Kitty. Can you tell me why the camp is here in a desert? How come?"

I asked many times, but no one ever gave me an answer. I was ignored. They acted like I was not there. Now, I know I am small and some people, like that soldier, acted like they did not see or hear me, but I was disappointed. I really spoke up just like my teachers and Granma taught me. I have to remember that they have to look down at me to answer. But some didn't even bother to look to see me. I was always trying to eat and grow higher and bigger.

"Our apartment," Dad said, "is in a block between the completed barracks and those still being built. They said the camp has not been entirely completed yet. Our remaining luggage will reach us later today, I hope."

We followed Dad and Mom to a block of barracks. He said each block had seven barracks on each side with the mess, lavatories and washroom barracks in the middle. Our apartment was on the west side of the camp, about halfway from the administration buildings where we were registered.

It was hard because the dusty wind never stopped. We were in two of the apartments because of the size of our family. Dad decided that Michio and Eichi would take one and Mom, Dad, Tomiko and me would take the other, it seemed bigger.

Much later, Eichi cut a doorway between the two apartments so we did not have to go outside to see each other. There was nothing in the apartments except iron cots and dust that came in through the floor cracks.

"The lumber for the flooring is not fitted and is obviously young green lumber which has warped, it is not tongue and groove, really cheap construction. And, the barrack has no skirts around it," Eichi explained.

"What do you mean skirts?" I laughed.

"Each barrack is raised off the desert, but should have protection, that is, skirts blocking the wind from coming in our place through the flooring. Of course, that is too late now. They said the barrack would be completed soon. We have no inside walls or ceilings," Eichi said.

He had performed carpentry and building work part time when he was in school. So had Michio, both later volunteered with Dad to help other inmates complete the remaining camp blocks and barracks.

"Just like at Tanforan, the basic living facilities were done without any respect or care for even decent living in mind," Mom concluded.

"Why did they go so far out here to make all these ugly buildings? I think they just not like us." I said.

"What about that big hole in each apartment?" Michio asked.

"Those are for the stoves, which are also coming soon, we hope," Dad added.

"But why did they let us come here when parts of the camp are not finished? And, how will we be protected from the cold? It's already getting chilly. That black paper for outer walls is no protection," Mom said.

Eichi said that it was construction paper that likely would be our permanent outer wall.

"The WRA says that the army is responsible for construction of the barracks in accord with regular minimal military specifications and requirements. But the trouble is that it does not meet any living requirements of any place where civilians live, only temporary barracks for the military. That means that they violate every state housing code in the U.S.A.," said Eichi.

He added that the lumber used for the floors and elsewhere is called "green lumber". Meaning that it is not properly aged and will continue to contract, warp and generally not stand up to any building standards.

The wind seemed never to stop or even take a rest. It was hard to get used to the noise it sometimes made. Wind made it very hard for leaving the apartment to do anything, but we had to eat, go to the bathroom and wash clothes and later go to school and other important places.

The camp workers had dumped large bales of straw like those at Tanforan, which we had to use to fill burlap bags for mattresses. We had to work fast before the wind blew most of it away. Nice and lumpy, but not really for sleeping.

We never stopped sweeping dust out of the apartment. It came through the floors, the walls and the hole in the roof where the stove would be someday. When we did go out, we had to wear bandanas so the dust would not get in our noses, eyes and mouths. If we made it to the mess we had to worry about dust getting in the food.

The WRA had printed a warning telling us not to breath or swallow the dust, as it was not healthy. Tomiko read it out loud to everyone and then asked, "Why then did they put us here? Didn't they even see that is what was happening in this desert?"

One day in the mess hall I heard some little kids talking, "Oh mom, we don't like Japan, can't we go back to

America, please?"

"Those little kids are really right, we might not ever get back to America," Tomiko said.

After more than a week the wind stopped a little. I went outside to see where we were, but it was so hard. As far as I looked there were more and more buildings like ours. I just was not sure how far it was or where it ended. Where we were, there was seven barracks on each side of the three middle buildings for the latrines, mess and washing barracks. In one direction, to the east we were the second block next to the edge of a clear area and fence. In the other direction, to the west, the barracks were just too far that I hardly could see that side of the fence that surrounded the camp.

I started walking to the distant fence. It seemed like all day. The further I got north, more barracks were not even finished, but more families were still coming to the camp. I think I saw Dad and then Eichi working on the newer ones. Several times on my way back to the apartment I thought I saw some little animals, but they were so fast and seemed scared of me. Later I was told they were wild rabbits or prairie dogs, but because we were in a desert I never was able to see many. I was told they were scavengers, food hunters, very sad and disappointing. They looked so cute. Then I learned that being wild they might have diseases.

There were lots of families and kids I recognized from Tanforan, but did not see any of the friends I had met. There were so many people that I wondered if I would ever get to see them, my friends, or meet new friends. I finally reached the far fence and crossed a little field. I think it was about noon, the sun was getting hot and I could not see my shadow. I saw also that even some of the fence was still being completed. I think some people were walking around outside. I didn't know if they were from the camp or soldiers, they were so far away. Along the way I saw little whitish shells and some chipped rocks. The rocks were broken but some had nice shapes that I thought someone had made. Later I found that they were parts of the heads of arrows.

I learned that the shells were from a big lake that died very long ago and now the camp was a part of it. The fence had light poles and big towers with soldiers in some of them. The fence also had barbed wire just like I first saw on the fences in Tanforan.

I was tired from walking and sat near the fence. I looked at the far mountains, which seemed so little. Like they were just tiny toy hills. There was nothing but kinda flat land that seemed to go forever. The mountains, so far away, were just like Grandma, our friends and home, so far away.

I thought about Hilo and Hawai'i. All that past, I guess that was what Tomiko called being "home sick". Then I remembered the word the teacher had mentioned in summer school: "*natsukashi-mi*", which means longing for the past. I hope our home does not stay forever in the past, so far away. We all, the family, still hope to go back there again, maybe soon.

I walked farther along the fence, but decided to start back to the apartment, it was getting very hot. I still saw more people just coming into the camp. There were sure a lot of kids, but I still could not find any of my friends.

The sky was turning yellow-brown. I was hungry, but was not sure how far I had gone. I saw what I thought was our block and got in a mess line. My family was not there. I ate anyway. When I went back out, I noticed the sky was really pretty, orange and reds, and purples. I kept walking, looking for our barrack.

"Kitty, where have you been?" It was Michio. "Mom was worried, we ate already and Dad and Eichi were just going to look for you."

"I went down to the far fence," pointing in the direction I had come from. "People are still coming to the camp. I was looking for friends."

"Rika, was looking for you." It was Tomiko, "She lives just in the next block. And so do her brothers. (I knew why she was smiling, she liked one of the brothers who was about her age.) Isn't that nice? Mom was a little worried about you."

"Did you see the nice sunset, it's sure better than all the dust all day," I answered.

Our stove had been delivered, but it was just sitting in front of the apartment with all the others in the barracks around us. Michio, Dad and Eichi had been collecting extra lumber so some furniture could be built.

That night I got to visit Rika. I showed her the shells I had collected. "Oh guess what?" said Rika. "I found some too, and these," she also had some of the broken stones like I found. "My dad says they are parts of arrow heads." Her father taught beginning history at the college in San Jose.

"Those are from probably the Ute or Shoshone Indians who used to live in Utah and Colorado. Now the shells are much older, many thousands of years, when this place used to be a large lake," Rika's father said. "I believe that you girls can even find some arrow heads that are intact."

"I have a roll of heavy thread I got in school in Tanforan. It was for crafts and we could use it to string our shells. Mom says it is too heavy to sew with," Rika suggested.

We made a plan to go soon to look for more shells and possibly some arrowheads, but the dust storms started again. We also wanted to find the barracks that would be our school, but it would be some time before we could do much outside. It was also getting colder at night and we heard that there might be rain coming. We still did not have either of the stoves hooked up and no interior walls or ceilings in the apartments.

Dad and Eichi were working hard to help the completion of barracks where other new internees were in need of completed apartments. Mom was able to get some work in the mess with meal preparations. Each block needed persons from their barracks to help with meals. Tomiko and Michio were also assigned to be kitchen helpers.

Mom said the meals were some improvement over those at Tanforan, but still not much variety.

"Each of us must work to make meals from very limited supplies. We had to persuade the administration to supply more variety. We have some here who are gifted in Japanese cuisine.

Tomiko and I wish to learn more. Especially since Tomiko wants to possibly become a chef," Mom said.

Mom hunted for a long time from block to block, to find a person who made tofu. She finally met a very elderly woman who wrote out the recipes for tofu making. "It turned out to be very simple, except that it will be a while before the mess has adequate refrigeration," Mom said.

We finally received real mattresses. They were that army color Mom called, "drab green and ugly." We scattered the straw around the barracks and used the burlap for room dividers. The mattresses were not as nice as those at home. I still missed home and wanted to go back.

Dad with others helped to open the first camp coop. Mom also helped with this job. As elsewhere, the wages were very low and the work was long and hard. I wished I could have helped.

The nights kept getting colder and there were still no inner walls. We got the stoves in the apartments, but had to still wait for roof material to seal each stove stack.

"We have to be careful when the stack is sealed, a woman was burned when some of the hot sealing pitch from the roof came through while it was being installed," Dad warned. "It was the second time that an accident has happened. Why couldn't the authorities wait until the camp was entirely completed before sending thousands of us to be imprisoned here with such inadequate living facilities?"

Eichi laughed, "That camp administrator insists that we be called residents and still denies that we were interned and not simply locked up. He is very mad when we call this as a concentration camp. He's from somewhere in the east, like Boston. My friend who works in the camp headquarters says he stays very aloof and does not deal on a first person basis with those of us he calls residents."

"Tomiko and I were able to get extra blankets from the warehouse," Michio reported. "Everyone is supposed to be issued extras due to the weather. There are also some surplus jackets from the army. The same color as the blankets," he said.

"But the sizes are really for big people. What do kids wear?" I asked. "And those army blankets, just like the first ones given to us in Tanforan are warm but scratchy."

We met a woman who was a professional seamstress who had volunteered to sew jackets for children after many of the surplus ones were cut up. Tomiko, Michio and I helped her take jackets apart and cut into sizes for the kids. It was fun, but tiring. I could not keep up with the others, but still did enough for four jackets.

It was a few days later that we got some rain. It was not very much, but we had to keep dumping water when it came in through the roof. It was a good thing that Mom had some of those big cans from the mess. The rain replaced some of the dust, but then there was mud.

"The camp was not sufficiently planned for simple drainage. The desert soil is an alkali which does not absorb much moisture," Dad said. "I have heard that the camp administration and the WRA are planning on bringing soon a variety of shrubs and trees to be planted over the entire camp. The trouble is, they may not take due to the soil and the lack of sufficient water. We barely have enough water to drink, wash with, and use for wastes."

I found the school for the primary kids, but it was just an empty building. No walls, ceilings or stove. Some of the kids I met said a teacher was coming soon, but knew nothing about desks or school supplies. Just like me, they didn't want to wait, looking to return to school as soon as possible. The schools had also been interrupted when all of us were taken away and locked up.

The regular camp staff workers installed the stoves. They were smoky at first and Michio showed Tomiko and me how to turn ours up or down.

"Is there going to be enough coal? That pile outside is small," I said.

"We hope to get more. You are right to be concerned. It is going to get colder. I heard the temperature could drop below zero," Eichi answered.

"Dad, what does hakujain mean? Some kids called the office workers that," I said.

"It means Caucasian."

"But what does that mean?" I asked.

"Well, it's actually a technical word that is used to mean a white person, like most Anglo-Americans or Europeans."

"Ok, but I don't understand why there are those kinds of names for people? That is confusing to me. It is just like people calling me both Japanese and American, you know, Japanese-American. Isn't it enough just to call us Americans?" I asked.

"Oh Kitty, what you are really asking is why are we here? It is something that we can do nothing about nor worry about," Dad answered. "We are here now and must live here and survive."

I thought for a long time what Dad said, then remembered what Mr. Omori said about 'shi kata ganai' and my problem of not seeing differences in the kids at school and Tomiko saying that I had to figure it out for myself. Mr. Omori said to keep seeing with my heart and not my eyes.

"Kitty, wake up. We gotta go to school," Tomiko was staring at me with a big smile. "Mom just got notified that the primary school would be opened today so we have to register and maybe meet our teacher."

I was so excited that I ate too fast that morning and nearly got sick.

The school had only benches. Hundreds of kids were waiting in line. Each of us received papers for our parents from two women and a man who we found out was in charge of the schools. The women were teachers. They were from the housing area where other camp headquarters workers lived. It was a little disappointing because school was still being organized with little classroom equipment and few teachers.

At first my class was combined with three other grades, first through third. There was just one teacher and she was only part-time for a couple days. Then one of the camp women who had some teaching experience came to our combined class. We sat on wooden benches, but still, I was happy. In my class there were nineteen kids who had finished one-half of the second grade. Plus there were second graders just starting. We had only half days until all classes were completed.

"We have some good news," Dad said. "Grandmother is coming tomorrow afternoon."

The family all worked hard to have the inside of the apartment completed, including the inside walls and ceiling. Thanks to Dad and Eichi, the job was done in time.

"We had to ask at least four times just to get the extra bed for Grandma, and they were annoyed, as if it was a special privilege just to ask. It was their job and responsibility," Eichi reported.

I was crazy with excitement. Mom and Dad said I could go to the gate to greet Grandma. Michio would arrange for her luggage.

A few days later I arrived at the gate early and waited for the bus. She was not on the first bus. I cried. The gate guard told me another bus would be arriving an hour later. Finally the second bus arrived. I watched as people got off. Then I saw Grandma. She was just standing beside the bus. The driver helped her as they walked slowly to the gate.

But why was she walking so slowly? She looked kind of

weak. My heart jumped. I was worried, but happy to see her. At first it was just a little hard to recognize her, had it not been for her nice blue overcoat. Grandma was older now, but I prayed to myself that things would be different and we would now all be one happy family together. I ran through the gate as she stood there alone smiling. I started crying.

"Oh, *Sobosan*, I'm so happy you are here, we really missed you and we love you so very much." I was looking up at her, hugging her legs and crying.

She looked down at me, and smiled, "Oh Miyako, our Kitty, thank you for meeting me. You have grown some. Here I'll wipe your tears. Now let's go home, you may show me the way."

I took her arm. I was ever so happy I could not help my crying. We very slowly made our way across the camp. I told her what had been happening since San Francisco. She was quiet, just listening. I could tell she was tired from her travels. I was so excited I just kept talking and hoped she didn't mind. It had been a long day and the afternoon sky was changing.

Fading into many colors. Blending from yellow, orange and then a red that darkened until it went from reddish black, then really black. We reached our block. I was losing my breath. We stopped in front of our apartment. We looked up as millions and millions of stars just burst out of all the night sky, it took away our breaths. Everything was quiet and very still.

"Oh look, Kitty!" Grandma whispered, as she held me,

"see how the heavens have welcomed us home?"

With the entire family together, things seemed better, but from that night on, it began to get even colder. Gradually the rain and mud changed to a little snow that was icy, making it difficult to walk. A lot of the time we would hold hands when walking anywhere. It was hard getting used to all the new and rapidly changing weather. Remembering and longing for San Francisco, so different, I still wanted to go home.

Finally, by the last of October, we were able to attend school all day. While sitting on benches we used boards left over from construction to write our lessons. It was funny because you had to hold your knees still to write, and I was still learning cursive writing and not printing. One day we received a surprise when desks came.

Soon it became too cold and the stoves were not enough so the teacher let us return home early. She was reprimanded for that. I am not sure what happened. I only know that she was ok. Later the rooms were better insulated, but some days it was still too cold, and school was closed on those days.

One day, Dad took me aside. He seemed very serious. "I know your little secret. That panda of yours was lost."

"Oh Dad, I am so much ashamed. I've missed it, but I've been trying to be a big girl too."

"Oh no, being a big girl does not mean giving up something or someone you love. You are still a big girl and certainly not a baby. Here, I have a small present for you. It may not be quite as nice as the panda you lost, but it's still something."

It was a little panda, the same black and white stuffed animal. I took it in my hands and squeezed it. It looked just like the pictures in magazines of big pandas, but small of course, a white head with black paws wide open, waiting to be hugged and to hug you back. I was so excited and wanted to cry. I reached over and hugged dad while holding the gift.

"Oh thank you. So you think it's OK for me to still keep it like when I was little? It's just like the one I had, and just as cute. I love you Dad, thank you, thank you. I promise I won't lose this one. It's small enough. I can even hide it."

He hugged me and explained, "Sure Kitty, never be ashamed to have a friend or companion just for yourself. I had a favorite toy when I was just your age and older. I will see that no one teases you about it. Are you going to name the panda?"

"Oh yes, I'll call him, Panda."

Along with the rain, snow, and cold, we had food shortages. There was a rationing of fresh milk for kids under five.

"Powered milk is OK for me. It is the only kind we have had anyway, it is just lousy tasting, that's all," I said.

The food shortages, off-and-on, lasted until almost spring.

One day I watched while an elderly man was busy in the

washroom making a wooden tub out of some of the surplus wood. It was a *furo* – a Japanese bathtub. I had remembered seeing one in Hilo behind a house that belonged to an older Japanese man. It was a tradition among Issei men and some women. It was a long tub, about three feet long, for one person to use after showering with nice hot water. But, because of coal shortages and water being mostly scarce I don't remember how often it was used. I never got to try it myself.

Grandma had to visit the doctor at the hospital, which still was unfinished. She was never quite the same since Texas. When she arrived in the women's internment camp in Texas she was sick, but was not able to see a doctor for almost two weeks even though she was older. Therefore, she was not well enough to later return to her family due to sickness that developed because of the delay in receiving medical treatment.

Tomiko and I often spent several days at home missing school because of colds. The school administrator said we had to get a nurse's approval before we could return to class. It took a long time to get to the hospital for a checkup each time we were absent. It was hard since most kids or parents had a difficult time going back and forth to get approval from the nurse at the hospital. Then, after a protest meeting, parents and teachers persuaded the administration to change the procedures so a nurse could be at the school to examine students and approve their return to school.

"It took meetings several times to convince the school heads to understand what we were talking about," Mom said. "Why couldn't they get someone with some experience and not some inane bureaucrat to run the schools and hospital?"

The lines to the mess were always such a long cold wait in the rain, wind and snow. The dust in between rain or snow was still bad. I got tired of wearing bandanas and having to wash them out so many times. Having to go to the mess during winter was continually difficult. Dust, rain or snow or all of it would make eating a hardship. Bandanas, coats and hats had to be worn and then removed and reused continually. Everyone wished they could eat meals only in their apartments.

We did not have the money yet to get a hot plate so we could make our own tea, soup, miso, or snacks. We wanted so much to go home where we had the right to do what we wanted, including eat in private.

Our school class was given a list of students at another camp. Manzanar in California was seeking pen pals. I found one student who interested me. Her name was Marta, an orphan. She had lived with a family, but because the family was not of Japanese ancestry, the authorities removed her from her legal parents and had her interned there in the so-called Orphans' Camp.

Marta was very unhappy and missed her family who had adopted and raised her since she was a baby. But the government did not approve of any Japanese-American living with a Caucasian family and so Marta was interned because of her ancestry. I learned that there were others taken under similar circumstances.

I was excited and wrote to her, introducing myself. I gave

my letter to our teacher, Miss Hart. It was sent with the other letters through the WRA to Manzanar camp. I wrote about our camp, where I had been, San Francisco and Hawai'i and asked about Marta and her family and her camp.

It was about a month later that Miss Hart gave me a letter from Marta. She was happy to write. She lived in the orphanage with others who had no family. She wanted to know all about my family and the camp. There were other things in her letter that had been blacked out. Miss Hart was told that some activities at her camp were not allowed in letters. When I mentioned this to Dad and Eichi they said that it may have also been about the troubles between the inmates, nearby local authorities and camp authorities.

"It should not have been censored, we heard the news on the radio and it was in the newspaper from Salt Lake City," Eichi said.

"But is there anything we can do?" I asked.

"Well Kitty, just cheer her up, but don't talk about the censor or the troubles. You might get her to tell you about activities in and around her camp and you can do the same here," Eichi said. "Just try to stay in touch so she is not isolated. That can hurt someone like her. She never should have been separated from her family. We have heard of other children who were separated for racial reasons like her. That was obscene and illegal."

Grandma was able to help with students at our school who were having troubles in their studies. She had worked in Hawai'i and San Francisco as a teacher before she retired to work with Grandfather. It was good to walk with her and Tomiko to school. She was very popular with the kids because of all the stories she told in the school and at the library.

One day I was asked to give the Pledge of Allegiance. During it I forgot it was the 10th of December 1942. When I finished I just stood there for a while and ran to my desk and cried.

"Kitty, what is the matter? It was perfect," Miss Hart asked.

"I was thinking about San Francisco and what happened to me on my birthday there. I still sort of miss it there, but I am also happy here." I could not really say anything more about what made me cry, it just came out. I just felt sad and then happy. Later, when I was in bed that night, I felt better about things, but could never forget what happened a year ago.

I was happy and safe, even if we were so far from home and so cold, or *samui*. (I had just learned a new Japanese word. I think that is the right word for cold.)

It was good when the library opened because I could see the librarian, the teacher I had known at Tanforan. She and Grandma were able to help more of the new and younger kids who needed help when their older sisters and brothers were in school.

Gradually they got some books from the Delta schools and finally the Tanforan library books arrived. Delta was the nearest town, about 50 miles from the camp.

Dad, Mom and Eichi have been going to some meetings for our block, but are not happy because Issei internees are not supposed to participate as leaders. The WRA says the reason is that they are aliens.

"That is totally wrong, they are our elders and should be accorded respect. The WRA is working against us and dividing people. I suggest we ignore the administration and continue to work and participate with our Issei. I also feel we have *giri*, the moral obligation to them," Dad urged.

Our family, being able to get work, received very small wages. Just like Tanforan, the pay for a month was about fifteen dollars. Teachers and doctors made a little more. That was still not much since the government spent thirty-one cents a day on food for each of us.

Throughout the rest of winter there were more food and even coal shortages. Dad and others tried to get extra food later to make up for the shortages, but they never were successful. There were also rumors that besides the food and coal, other supplies in the camp warehouses disappeared and became part of the black market there in Utah.

It was near the holidays, so Michio wanted to make mochi, but we had to wait for the rice. After getting together with all those in our block we had enough to make a little for everyone. The only problem was trying to filter out the chlorine in the camp water. Some water had been collected from the rains. It was OK but no one thought the taste was quite the same as when all of us were free and enjoyed mochi at home.

Sometimes it would be so cold at night that I would snuggle up in my covers and not move. Mom told me that by not moving my own heat would help me keep warm. It worked sometimes, but did not stop the shivers. That is when Tomiko and me would cuddle up together. I was happy then to have some warm scratchy army blankets.

Once I went home to our house. I found it warmer. I could even see the sun. But Tomiko woke me because I was talking to Panda about all the flowers and chimes. "Sorry, I just wanted to tell Panda about our little garden."

She asked if I was feeling all right. "Please just go to sleep Kitty and try not to make any noise when you dream," she asked. I tried to tell her I was just going back to our home, but she would just look at me, smile, shake her head a little and go back to sleep. I don't think she believed me.

Some Issei neighbors were taken to the administration offices because the camp security said they were chanting in Japanese during a New Year celebration. They were also asked if they were practicing Shinto, which was prohibited by the WRA. The Issei said they were chanting a Zen Buddhist prayer. The block committee complained of the harassment, stating that such a prohibition was religious bias and none of the camp administration's business. The Issei continued chanting in Japanese, which the committee supported.

The camp director's office reviewed summaries of each block committee's meeting and made so-called corrections in them for calling Topaz a "concentration camp." But the committee informed the director that in October the president had stated publically that the relocation centers were "concentration camps" during a press conference. The camp director did not respond, ignored us and continued to correct their minutes as he saw fit.

In February, I moved up to the 3rd grade in school. "Kitty, you have worked very hard on your studies. If you continue, you may be able to skip half a year and when fall comes, become a 4th grader. But only if you work very hard," my teacher said.

"Oh thank you, Miss Hart. I will really work and study hard."

A week later, after learning much about Abraham Lincoln, the Gettysburg Address and his Emancipation Proclamation that freed Negroes from slavery, I had questions about the idea of everyone being created equal and how that worked for all of us in the camp and the people I had seen on the train and in San Francisco. When my brother's friends tried to join the army after Pearl Harbor, only the white friends were allowed to join, but not his Japanese-American and Negro friends. Where I went to school in San Francisco, all my teachers are white and in what is called *Nihon Mache* (Japan Town) all the teachers were Japanese or Chinese. On the train, all the dining and other service persons were Negro, and all the army soldiers on the train and in Topaz and Tanforan were white. At Topaz, all teachers, administration workers and soldiers were white and stayed in a separate living place that is nicer than where we had to stay, and their wages are way more than anybody here who works in camp where we are interned because of our ancestry. And all the teacher assistants, our librarian and local inmates are

Japanese-Americans.

I wrote all that out, it took me a long long time, and I gave it to my teacher, but she said she could not give me an answer. I wrote it because she had asked me what I thought of what I had studied and learned about Mr. Lincoln and what he said and what happened.

Sometime later, the man in charge of the schools came and asked me who wrote my report and questioned me. I told him I did. He just looked at me and shook his head like "no" and asked me the same question a couple more times. I told him I wrote all of it and that I did not understand why he shook his head. He did not answer my question. He just took some notes and left. I don't think he was happy. I was afraid I was in trouble. I thought I had studied well and wanted to know if what I wrote was OK and if I had figured out everything correctly.

About a week later, Dad, Mom and Grandmother were called into the camp administrator's office. I knew I must be in trouble.

The next night with the family Dad told me, "Kitty, what you wrote and questioned about has been like that for a very long time. Please tell us before you ask any more such questions of your teacher. She is not allowed to comment on your questions. It is therefore difficult for her because what you asked has gone on for many decades, almost forever. We know that the questions are important and that is the way things are and the reasons why we are locked up in this camp are wrong, illegal and confusing.

We are not mad at you in the least, but secretly very proud

of you and happy about what you wrote. Just talk with us before you ask any more questions. No one is in trouble. But no one can do anything about it. The camp administrators are very afraid of all of us. So it's often best not to complain too much. We all have done that, maybe a little too much."

In early February, Eichi said he wanted to be included in the voluntary and active duty program to join the army.

"The government has now said that we can join. They are already allowing volunteers from the camps and also from Hawai'i to join."

Dad gave him permission. His birthday was in March. He would be eighteen and eligible to join on his own. Mom and Grandma both said they would rather he didn't join.

"I know, but there are guys here who also feel like I do, we should do our patriotic duty, we are at war," he said in reply to Mom and Grandma's reluctance.

"Yeah, but they locked us up and now they need us to help them. I see that all you guys will be in units of only Japanese-Americans. Just like what they have been doing to us, segregating us because of our ancestry, which isn't right," Michio said.

"But they will still be representing all of us for a good cause and they are needed. It is wartime," Dad said.

Eichi gave Tomiko and me all his defense and war savings stamps (which would someday add up to buying a war savings bond). Each class in the two camp schools had a competition between classes about the war savings stamps. We could not wait to take them to school so our class' goals could be met.

There was a going away party for all the young men in each block. But there were also many neighbors in the camp who did not approve of them going.

Arguments about joining a segregated unit or division, was one objection. "The government gave no alternative and we have found that Negroes and other non-whites are also segregated," Dad said.

"But that is no excuse," one neighbor said. "Why should we believe anything good will come of it? Look how so many of us Issei have worked long and hard for years, and now have nothing. We have loved this country for naught. I have been denied citizenship, but have given to this country. You should not let your son go. He might even fight against Japan. Don't you understand? His country locked him up like all of us. Even if in our hearts we are loyal, we have all been treated like the enemy. It's all so crazy. I am no friend of Nihon. But what am I to do?"

I could see that Dad only looked at him and nodded yes. I felt sad and funny because our neighbor was right. I wanted to cry, I hoped that we would still be friends and neighbors. I don't think Dad was very happy.

At the same time there were some other problems in the camp. In the middle of the night I could hear my parents, Grandma and Eichi arguing.

"Last night, did you hear them arguing?" I asked Tomiko

and Michio when we were eating breakfast before school.

"It was something about questions and a questionnaire all adults now have to fill out for the government," Tomiko answered.

"They kept talking about 'loyalty'. That's all I heard," Michio said.

In school, kids talked about their parents having similar arguments and discussions. Everything seemed confusing and there were many different opinions and information about loyalty. After a few days we met with other classes and one of the supervisors said the questionnaires were for every adult in the camp and that we should ask our parents and not disrupt classes. The superintendent was not happy and said that it was "not your business".

"What is it about loyalty?" one student asked. "My dad said it was about loyalty to America or Japan."

The superintendent frowned and did not reply to her. He did say that the WRA, who authored the questionnaire, will be sending representatives to each block council to explain everything.

Dad explained that a majority of the questions were routine, but two involved loyalty. "They are really meant for Nisei and Issei concerning loyalty to the United States and Japan. The whole thing is a screen to determine the eligibility of individuals to leave camp to join the military, go to college, or even work outside U.S. restricted zones.

But there is resentment over two of the questions,

numbers 28 and 29. Number 28 is directed mainly at Nisei, who are asked to confirm loyalty to the U.S government, and number 29 is directed to Issei to essentially denounce any loyalty to the Emperor of Japan. Immediately, you can see, there are complications. Things are not as simple as the WRA wants us to believe.

For all of us who are citizens, the question is insulting to have to reconfirm our loyalty to this country. The other is a dilemma for all our Issei neighbors because they are prohibited from being citizens, yet must now denounce the emperor of Japan in order to pledge allegiance to the U.S. The dilemma being that they would be without a country if they answer yes. The two questions have upset many people."

"Gee Dad, it is so confusing. Why didn't they ask about loyalty before they locked us all up? Are we not all on the same side in the war against Japan? What about that investigation they made before the war that said we are all loyal? It does not make much sense. I'm glad to just be a kid, and not have to answer any dumb questions," I said.

In the middle of spring, hundreds of small trees, shrubs and plants were delivered to the camp. Miss Hart announced, "Students will be responsible for planting trees around the school. Plants will also be provided for areas around the apartment barracks."

One of my school friends, David asked, "What about the bad desert soil? I remember that Rika's dad said that the soil is alkali, one reason the desert we are living in is barren."

"I will ask about that," Miss Hart replied.

I remember when I first tried to find out why the camp was built in the middle of the desert and that I was ignored. "I don't think they are going to give our teacher any answer," I told David and the other kids.

We all worked hard after school and sometimes during recess on planting. As did everyone all over the camp planting the trees, shrubs and garden plants around the barracks. Digging into the hard alkali soil was difficult. Unfortunately, even though they were given extra water, almost all of them did not grow.

By early summer only a few grew very slowly. They had to have extra water and shade due to the hot sun. I remembered something else that Rika's dad had also mentioned, that the high chlorine in the water did not help.

One day, while wandering through the camp looking for arrowheads and shells, I slipped and fell and I got a nasty scrape, which hurt. I remembered where Dr. Namamura lived. My family and neighbors met him when we were first registered and examined. I found his apartment and I showed him my arm, skinned, dirty and bloody. I was afraid he would be mad at me, but he was kind. I liked him. He cleaned it, but it really stung and I had to grit my teeth and look away. Then I peeked at him, he was busy looking at my arm and then caught me looking at him and smiled.

"I heard from some of your friends that you are called little dirty face, why is that?" I stared at him and did not answer. How come he said that? How did he know?

"I know your name, it is Kitty. Some of your friends have also come to me for cuts and scrapes. They told me your nickname."

"Thank you," I said. I didn't know what else to say. I was crying a little from when he cleaned my arm. I was surprised when he gently wiped my tears. Then I smiled at him. He gave me some of his wife's tea. Before I realized it, I started asking him about what he was doing in the camp and why he was not working in the hospital. He explained that there had been an extra doctor there and he was glad to just be living near the rest of us in the camp.

"I don't care to work for those who locked us up. But I am happy to help anyone who is in need. Just like you."

We talked some more and I asked some questions about medicine. Including what he put on my arm and what he did as a doctor. We became friends and he even gave me a book on medicine to read. He wanted me to take care of myself so when I played I would not get infected. He was interesting. I went back for more books to read too, even though they were really difficult, but I liked to read them anyway.

During spring and summer Michio played baseball with other boys his age. He was a pitcher. "I'm not really good, because all I can do is throw it side arm and as fast as I can. It fools and confuses the batters though," he told us.

We all went to watch him from time to time. He also still liked to study electronics in the junior high school's science laboratory and electric shop.

Late one night in April, we heard that someone had been shot. It was an elderly man, Mr. Wakasa, who was hard of hearing. He had been walking along one of the fences when a tower guard shot him. The guard claimed the old man was attempting to escape and ordered him to stop before shooting him. Mr. Wakasa died and the guard was exonerated. Some neighbors said they heard no order by the guard. The camp administrator denied permission for a funeral, but one was held anyway.

"It was very sad, many brought paper flowers and made little paper cranes. I heard there were over one thousand flowers and cranes," Tomiko said.

I learned the word,"*yoku-nai*," that day. It means, "not right." It was about what happened to him. I hoped that I could remember that word so I might use it again some other time.

After the funeral, we heard that there were some protests concerning the shooting, but after a time, nothing more was said, unfortunately.

Soon after the shooting and funeral, signs were all along the fence warning persons not to violate it.

I stood near the fence and stared at the hills and mountains so far away. I wondered if anyone could really run away from the camp and not die from lack of water and food, or the heat in the day and cold at night.

"There was no place anyone could go out there and survive," Miss Hart said. I agreed with her, our camp is too many miles from nowhere.

"Then the guard towers were not for our protection, but just for shooting us," David remarked. Miss Hart did not respond.

Since the time when the questionnaire was issued, many inmates all over Topaz camp began to organize into various protest groups concerning the loyalty questions.

Large groups in each block attempted to petition the camp administration. The petitions were refused and initially the groups were ignored. Then the administration, along with the WRA began making statements and warning them to stop protesting.

"I have learned that the WRA now considers the protesters to be disloyal and anyone who responded in the negative, or those who asked for any clarification of the two questions, or in many instances were willing to answer them if they were given some clarification that they would be given back their civil rights," Dad reported to the family and at the block meeting.

"You mean that anyone who questions the Questionnaires and raises the issues of civil rights is disloyal?" asked one of the neighbors in the block.

"Yes, that is our understanding of what the WRA means. I don't think it is a rumor," Dad answered. "They are saying that by raising issues of civil rights we are not complying with the WRA's questions and government policy."

"Why would they be called disloyal for just asking for their rights or not answering a question? That is confusing and I do not understand. I thought it was ok to ask?" I said.

Hearings were convened for those persons who applied for transfer out of the prohibited zones to work or attend a school. During the hearings, some raised again questions concerning redress. That is, restoring their civil rights if they answered the questionnaire in the affirmative. The hearing leader refused to answer those particular questions and was gaveled out of order and ordered to stop mentioning civil rights.

We all agreed, something different was going on. "Those questions are loaded," Grandma said.

Toward the end of spring, another serious problem arose. "A group of young men were given draft notices but have refused to comply with the deadlines and have been placed under house arrest by the camp security. I think that the WRA is now involved, but information is hard to get. The camp administration is considering them to be breaking the law. It is serious," Dad said.

During the early summer I heard about a man who had been feeding crumbs to little birds who had come to his windowsill. His name was Mr. Adachi. I visited his apartment on many afternoons and watched, for the longest time, as the birds would gradually trust him and then eat out of his hand.

Finally, he invited some of us kids to participate, including me. I was very scared, but excited. He showed me how to hold my hand very slowly and carefully with some crumbs. I was still excited and nervous, but after a long time, one bird got really near and then when there were no crumbs except in my hands it jumped onto my hand, but I must have moved just a very little. He got scared and left. I was sad, but Mr. Adachi told me to very slowly try again. It still took many tries, but a few days later a bird stayed until all the crumbs were gone and did not fly away. I even tried to whisper to it. I was so happy I almost cried.

"The birdie likes me, don't he?" I whispered again.

When I returned that night I told everyone about the little bird and what I did. I was so happy that I hugged everyone. I just hoped they were not tired of me telling them about the little bird.

One nice thing was that some young adults were actually able to relocate to colleges after attending the hearings on the loyalty questions in early summer.

Grandma said that it was the lone positive aspect of the questionnaire. "It was sad that the main part had created militancy and outrage where none had before existed. All over the illegal treatment we were subjected to since we were interned." She concluded.

At the end of July we had a Buddhist celebration and a bon dance and ceremony in remembrance of our loved ones who passed away.

I talked quietly to Grandfather, "I hope you are all right and happy. It is good you did not have to live through the winter. I will always miss you. Thank you, I love you, your Kitty."

During spring and early summer Topaz camp had visitors, various birds and animals. The birds must have flown all the way from the ocean. Prairie animals showed up that were very cute, but we were warned not to touch or collect them. They were wild and were not always friendly. A camp aid said that the animals could have hurt us or we could have harmed them. We definitely did not like the mosquitos that also came with spring and early summer.

Then there was a new problem. Our parents were saying that we would be going to another camp. "Mom, Dad, Grandma, do we really have to go to another camp?" I asked.

Mom said that the new camp was called Tule Lake in California, and there would be some internees, like our family, moving there from other camps as well as Topaz camp.

"But why?" I asked.

"It is because of the questionnaire," Mom replied at the family meeting. "Specifically questions 28 and 29."

"We had to make a very difficult decision," Grandma said. "On my questionnaire I answered "no" to both question 28 and 29 because being an Issei I'm not allowed to be a citizen, but I will not say anything about the Emperor of Japan. If I did disavow him I would have no country. It may have been the place of my birth, but I was only an infant when I left. Not, of course a choice of my own. In my heart I am completely a citizen of America and owe my allegiance to this country, even if I am denied citizenship because of my ancestry. The cruel consequence of being in the dilemma of those questions is that I have been declared a disloyal, and must transfer to Tule Lake."

"Your Dad and I refused to answer "yes" to one or both of the questions so we have also been declared disloyal, so we must transfer to Tule Lake," Mom explained. "We could have answered "yes" to both questions, and remained in Topaz camp, but we both feel that as citizens we do not now have to swear our loyalty to this country. We are already loyal citizens of this country and feel deeply that our loyalty should not now be in question. We did not disobey the government when they illegally interned our family."

"So, you two, Mom and Dad, are also considered disloyal? And so you, and the rest of us have to also go to Tule Lake?" Tomiko asked.

"Yes," Dad replied. "If we had both answered 'yes' to both questions, we would have been able to remain in Topaz and the family would have been separated and that would have been unthinkable. Besides, it would go against our consciences to answer yes to such deceptive questions."

I had studied very hard so that I could pass a test my teacher was going to give in the fall semester. If I passed I would be able to skip to the third grade, but with the new move coming up, I wasn't sure any of this would happen.

There were other things that I would miss by going to Tule Lake. Some good friends would be staying at Topaz. Also, there was a mountain camping trip sponsored by Delta citizens for the benefit of kids in the community and Topaz kids were invited. There was a place to swim, horses and hiking trails. I would also miss some of the teachers, the camp librarian and neighbors, the little birds and nice sunsets. But I would never miss the winter weather. I hated the cold, it was so unfair, just mean. Of course, nobody liked the wind.

There was a Ute gentleman I met on a field trip to the Delta library, and I was sad that I would never get to see him again when we left Topaz. I think his name was Sutonaw. He was small like us kids, and very elderly. His hair was very shiny white and he had the nicest smile. When we told him who we were and where we were from he bowed his head and smiled.

"It is very strange those people brought you to such a place. It is now more than just a desert but a place of no place. Our people would never live even nearby," he said.

"Do you mean it is haunted?" Rika asked.

"No, it is said that it has no life. That is sad. It is best a place to leave. Only the foolish would build such a place and is punishment to those forced to live there."

When I thought of what Sutonaw said, I felt good that we were leaving, but sad for all those, including my friends who would still be there. I knew it would remain a hard place, he was right.

On the morning that we were all leaving the apartment, with everything packed for the shipment I asked, "What about everyone staying? I'm gonna miss them so much." I started crying, I just could not help myself.

No one said anything and kept walking. I looked around, my friends were waving goodbye. I tried waving, but just kept crying. That darn wind was still blowing dust. Like that first day, it was covering everyone as we left the camp gate. The darn dust made my face all smeary.

"Oh Kitty, you should look at yourself, how can we clean you up now, we have to board the bus. Wipe yourself with your bandana, you are a mess," Mom said.

"I just don't care," I answered.

As we left Topaz camp and the bus started down the road toward Delta town I went to the back of the bus to look back that last time. It was about a year since we had arrived. Just like then, big clouds of dust. Gradually the camp seemed to fade away into the desert.

I felt sad, leaving behind all the families who were staying. I didn't know if I was crying to leave them, or glad to leave. It was a nice warm summer, but I couldn't forget that darn winter. Those freezing nights and the colds we all had. Grandma was better now, but she sure stayed a long time in the hospital. Mom said there were little kids and babies who died that winter. Topaz never could be a good place to live.

Before we left Topaz, we got a V-Mail from Eichi. He explained that during the war, letters from military were reduced to microfilm and printed on little "v-mail" to save paper and get to us faster, a really neat thing and easy to put with our things. He could not say where he was, but that there were a lot of new soldiers from Hawai'i in his training camp. He did not say when he would leave for the war. That was scary and worried all of us.

When the bus passed through Delta town I wished we could have stopped. There were nice people there who helped us. I would miss them just like I missed all my friends in Topaz camp. We had some happy times. Just hoped that Tule Lake would be better. We were going away and would not return. It seemed strange looking back and I sorta cried remembering things I wanted to forget, except friends I would miss. So I returned to my seat next to Tomiko, leaning on and hugging her. She just smiled at me and we both slept.

TRAIN TO CALIFORNIA

At the Salt Lake terminal we boarded a train going west toward California. Some friendly soldiers said that it would take about as long as the one we took from Tanforan to Utah. Except that the route would be different, what they called scenic. It was not as crowded. We had nicer seats and I got to sit by the window.

I liked staring out, letting dakine to go whizzing by, sometimes not really looking at anything. This time there was only a little part of the desert before we started through mountains and forests. I did not care much about where we were or what towns and places went by. Things just seemed different and I was happy to be there.

That's when I began to wish someday I could take my own train trip. Not on an old train with soldiers because we might do something bad. But a train trip just because. Go travel in a free country anywhere in America. Seeing places like I had seen in pictures and movies and even in some of the songs about different places. I could maybe say where I want to go and take some friends and maybe write to the family about all I had seen. Or we all could go because we wanted to, not be forced ever again.

Everyone said it was a free country, Mom, Dad, and teachers. But what is "being free?" Not locked up on this train and going to California, to another camp they call Tule Lake.

They were so wrong, the government, in locking us up. They knew it was wrong, what Dad said was illegal. So why did they let it happen? I think it was called prejudice, because of our ancestry. But they didn't ever tell us why it was a mistake. All we knew is that it happened. And we couldn't do anything about it.

We heard that some people don't like us being free like them? I wondered if we would ever get to talk to them and ask why? What does that mean when they say that only peoples like their race, color, religion and ancestry live free in America? Why?

All those times we said the Pledge of Allegiance, is there really "one nation indivisible"? Grandma says that means we are all together not separated. So how come we are not? I know it's not just us. Other people are separated because of their ancestry or color, like us.

So what does the Pledge really mean? Not indivisible but just maybe invisible. Is that us? Dad laughed when I said that. He said that was a funny pun. But that made me mad, I was serious.

Maybe they not say the same Pledge, but something different? Even when the words are the same? I can't understand, it's confusing to me.

I hugged Panda and told him, "Remember, whatever happens we will still take a trip like we want and not because someone said it was necessary."

We went to our garden. "See all the nice things, the trees, grass, flowers and the little tea garden. Oh look up, see the clouds and stars. Listen to the chimes tinkle and smell the free air. See the funny shapes the clouds make? Maybe if we keep looking up we can see another seagull like the one who came one day to Topaz camp. I don't miss camp, but hope I will see most of my friends again. I am so glad Dad found you. Grandma said just to remember the happy times, even for only one moment."

I remembered what the librarian said about Tule Lake being warmer then Topaz in winter. She was a good friend at Topaz and at Tanforan. I felt so sorry about her little son being so ill most of the time. They had been in the stables like us. But her little boy became sick. We were lucky none of our family was sick from whatever had been in there.

Days and nights seem to go by fast. I mostly slept and dreamed of home. Often I visited our little garden and the big park in the City. I was happy. I saw those little birds of Mr. Adachi. Not really his, but he was so nice to care for them and they seemed happy visiting him. He was, as Mom said, a little sanctuary in the desert. Maybe I would sometimes have a pet just like the birds I have seen in San Francisco and even at home in Hawai'i. They seem always to be happy and free.

All of a sudden the train's wheels started screeching and we slowed to a stop. Everyone started talking and Mom was calling Tomiko and me. But I did not answer because I knew our nice train trip had ended. I asked myself, why couldn't we just go home? It had been so long, I was afraid that I might have forgotten what it was really like.

We left the train and everyone boarded buses. We were

now in Northern California. A little later someone said we were near Tule Lake camp. I felt a little better about that. Being in California. It meant that we were near our home, well sort of. There were farms and trees and lots of grasses. I could see some little hills and smaller nearby mountains. The buses started moving. Tomiko was sitting next to me now. I was still tired and I laid my head on her shoulder, she was sleeping and I was just starting to close my eyes.

Then someone cried out: "Are we in Japan? I can see Mount Fuji."

"No, no, that is Mount Shasta, we are in California and our camp, Tule Lake, is just over there," a passenger answered and pointed.

TULE LAKE CAMP

Tomiko and I looked up to see a huge camp. But it was different. It was surrounded with big high fences. I could see many more guard towers than Topaz camp.

"This concentration camp, Tule Lake, is special," Dad had said. "It was reconstructed by the WRA as the segregated camp. Different from the remaining internment camps in the country. They are saying it is for "disloyal" internees."

I got a bad feeling. I saw near the camp a group of strange cars or trucks. "What are those?" I asked.

"Oh, they are army tanks, with gun turrets, and armored cars. It is a military encampment. Along with all their soldiers." someone answered.

"Why? What are they for? Is there a war here somewhere?" I asked.

"No, they are for us."

My heart jumped, "We gonna be killed by them?" I started crying, hiding my face in Tomiko's lap.

"No, I don't wanna die, we did nothing wrong." I was getting dizzy and started shaking.

When everyone began to leave the bus, I shook my head, I could not move. Just closed my eyes and curled up in a corner of the seat. Tomiko tried to pull me out.

"Please Kitty, I know you are frightened. I'll keep a hold of you. We have to leave the bus. Mom is just outside with Dad and Grandma. We cannot stay here. We gotta catch up with them!" she was yelling at me.

"No, this time I won't go to another camp. No more camps," I told her as I held on to something with my eyes shut.

"Kitty, get up and get off the bus!" It was Grandma's voice. I got up and left the bus, my eyes still closed. Then I felt her hugging me. I was still crying.

I stayed with her as the family registered. Then I finally opened my eyes. Standing, between Tomiko and Grandma just inside the camp gate, I told her I was sorry.

"Oh, it's all right, we are all a little scared," she said.

I smiled, looked up at her and said, "Grandma, it's not better, there is no freedom, not ever. They think we are the enemy."

"Kitty, you are right, but we are all here together, no matter what is happening," she said. "Now you go ahead with Tomiko and Michio, I'll be along with your mother and dad."

We had a long walk to our block. My eyes were still full of tears. All I saw were the rows and rows of long black tar-papered barracks like the camp we left. Except some had nice little gardens of rocks, flowers and vegetables growing, and there were some with little planted bushes and trees.

"Look," Tomiko and Michio spoke up, trying to cheer me. "It seems a little better here, no desert blizzard like when we first arrived in Topaz camp."

I was so glad to see all the growing things. I remembered all the hard work in Topaz camp trying to plant anything. Almost everything just dried up. It was a waste. I didn't believe the WRA knew what they were doing. They wasted money we could have had for food during the shortages.

"Maybe we can grow some of our own vegetables," I said.

When we found our apartment we had a nice surprise. The internees that went elsewhere left a table, sheets used to separate the beds and some shelves. The windows had curtains, and we found a little broom and some cleaning stuff.

"That was nice of them," Tomiko said, "we should find out their names and addresses. We can write and thank them."

Mom and Dad arrived later with Grandma. They had to get someone to give her a ride. The walk would have been too hard for her. I didn't think she was feeling very good. Mom said the nurse and then a doctor examined her and wanted her to have lots of rest.

Our parents were also happy with the new place. "Let's hope things now will be better," Mom said.

Grandmother went to bed early. Two weeks later she had to be taken to the camp hospital.

Dad said, "They could not even give her a room, just a bed in the hallway. There is no doctor right now. I hear that the one that was here has transferred elsewhere and another doctor was drafted into the military. Those fools, they make no sense. Why can't they plan ahead when they move so many people? Why don't they take into account the internees' needs first, as if they ever did?"

"But more important and serious, the WRA calls this concentration camp officially the Segregation Center for the entire country, as a result of pressure from Congress, the military and even the JACL. WRA's simple-minded bureaucrats that devised that questionnaire which demanded only simplistic questions, no thinking person could answer. Naturally the internees were dumbfounded, insulted, mistreated and punished. They attempted to respond by asking their own questions, such as the ongoing government civil rights violations. Our questions were a sincere attempt for clarification so we could answer the so-called loyalty questions. Instead we are "disloyal" and moved here for raising any question," Dad again concluded.

"I didn't know that it was against the law to simply question such ambiguities and disparities. I wonder where it is written in the law that a person cannot ask a question? And is it illegal to be precocious?" Mom wondered.

That same day I heard on the radio, "Tule Lake's population had increased by about 12,000 disloyal persons who were transferred from the other nine camps. Making it the largest penal camp in the WRA system."

"So Dad," I asked, "the radio says that we are disloyal. But I am not disloyal, nor our family. So is that just someone on the radio lying? And are we in a penal center, what is that?"

"Oh no, what you are hearing in that news is entirely false. No one here is "disloyal" and Tule Lake is not a penal camp. A legal penal colony is for convicted criminals," he answered. "You have been listening to dangerous propaganda. I'll have to explain that later when we can have a family meeting," he said.

A week later at our family meeting Mom complained, "At Topaz camp there was harmony among the neighbors. Things here are different here. Some of our neighbors want to know if we are "no no", "yes no", and all that. Most are very quiet, and keep to themselves. Others don't even smile or say hello. Maybe it's due to so many of us being recently moved from other camps," she said.

"This camp is much bigger and still growing with added barracks being built daily," Dad said. "We just have to give things a little time for everything to settle."

"The radio news and the papers tell lies that come from those groups who falsely said that we are the enemy and want us locked up permanently and deported. An example, unfortunately, is the community around this camp. It is very biased and has a prohibition against any non-white and non-Christian persons living or working here," he added.

"Well, that is why they really must be upset with all of us not being like them," Michio said.

About a week later, we went to our first block meeting. There we learned that about a year ago there were two labor strikes and protests about a shortage of food and, differences in salaries and other workers' problems. There were so many things I did not understand, and we were all worried. It was hard to sleep than night.

The block chairman explained, "The community outside our camp sees our protests as a threat to themselves. They have engaged in false propaganda accusing some of us of performing illegal acts and being disloyal to the country. The protests and strikes were violently putdown by the former camp administrator. He was later quietly transferred elsewhere."

Like when we first arrived in Topaz camp, I decided to explore Tule Lake camp. It was much bigger. The blocks and barracks seemed to go on and on and some were still being built. Beyond the big fences I could see many farms and fields. I found out that some were planted for our neighbors to work in outside the camp for our food. They were allowed outside along with the soldiers from the army encampment.

I could also see other fields of crops and farms far beyond the camp. There were railroad tracks off to the south and west, warehouses, other camp buildings, and the army encampment for the soldiers and guards. South of the camp was also a funny looking hill they said was called Castle Rock and just peeking beyond that was Mount Shasta.

I always wanted to visit that mountain. I had seen it on a map and pictures in the school library at home. It seemed to look down over all of California to the south. Now we were somewhere north, on the other side. I stared at it for a long time and thought of how far we were from San Francisco and our home. I wanted to go home. It still hurt every time I thought about home. We were happy there.

I met a lot of kids who didn't look like they were disloyal. Nor did they look like the enemy. Just us American kids. Some I talked to said that many neighbors wanted to go to Japan. Some talked about rumors that Nihon was winning the war. That was confusing because there had been news since last year that we were winning in the Pacific. Like at Mid-Way, where the Japanese Navy lost many ships, the news had said last year.

I asked myself, "What was true?" I don't think I understood everything. It was sometimes frightening. It didn't help that Tule Lake camp had so many armored cars, guard towers, and soldiers with guns watching us.

One day I asked Mom: "Is it OK if I visit Grandma, please, I miss her."

"Oh yes, that would be fine," replied Mom. "She has been moved to a room with other patients and would be happy to see you. Maybe it will cheer you up too."

Early that morning I visited the hospital and found Grandma.

"Kitty, what is the matter? You are so quiet and not smiling. Shouldn't you be in school now or soon?"

"Well yes, very soon, but I just don't care and not really understand dakine anymore. We will never go home. We are not free ever. Some people talk about going to Japan. Are they really winning the war? That is what some are saying. What will happen to us? People on the outside don't like us. Please Grandma. Promise we won't have to go to Japan. Some people that scare me say we must renounce our citizenship because of what has happened to all of us. Does renounce mean no more being a citizen? We have never been in Japan and we are at war with them. I am confused and afraid. What will happen?" I started to cry.

She took my hand and held it, "Just slow down and relax! Those are rumors, just rumors. We will not have to go to Japan. I will not allow it. But you are right. There are some here who are still upset, like you, over being locked up. Please cheer up. There is no need to cry. You are a brave American citizen and that is important. Your parents are not going to renounce their citizenship. I know it's very hard for you to not be depressed. Being here in camp is not easy for any of us. Remember, we cannot let those who wronged us get their way. We are all together, part of caring and loving families.

So Kitty, have faith, you are not going to give up on yourself. We are all counting on you. You will make us all very happy and proud. So go now. Study, you have too much work to do and should not be bothered by rumors and bad talk. When I see you again it will be good news, so promise me not to worry, you will do well."

"But why, Grandma, are some of them called "no-no" like you said you are?" I asked and cried again.

"Now calm down. I'm a "no-no" because I did not answer the questionnaire just the way the government wanted. Being a "no-no" is not some bad word. Nor does it mean I would give up. I would never leave any of you. I am still an American, even if they would not let me be a citizen. A number of those called "no-no", like the Kibei, those sent to Japan to learn the culture, are just like us, very right in their beliefs about being betrayed by America. But not all of us are so hasty to condemn. We know we have a much better chance here, despite all that has happened. We have *gaman*, to persevere, to hold on to ourselves, and not give up.

Now remember this, no one here is really disloyal. That is just a big lie. We are all loyal. As your dad said, it is just another deception by the WRA. So don't be afraid or dislike any of our neighbors. We must tolerate, love and respect them and try to understand their opinions and beliefs. They too are part of our greater family. Just remember, study, have faith and make us all proud."

"Yes, I promise Grandma, *Sobosan*, thank you, I love you."

When I returned, I told Mom that Grandmother was doing much better, and all about our talk. That made her smile.

"Now I am going to find out about my school."

I wandered until I found it and discovered that my teacher, Miss Hart, had transferred from Topaz camp. I started feeling better and excited to start school again.

There were some days before school would start so I decided to continue exploring. Tule Lake camp had wild grasses and cinder rock gravel everywhere, and like Topaz camp, there were shells. Shells like I had collected with Rika, but I had lost mine.

I wondered. "Why do I keep losing things? " I never used to lose anything until we left San Francisco. Had I done something wrong? I can't remember doing that before. Like my Panda I was given in Hawai'i. Then with the shells I found in Topaz camp.

I looked for friends from the other camps. But now there were so many more kids. I hoped that I could make new friends and not be shy and afraid when they talked to me. I kept thinking about Grandma. First they take her away and she gets sick because she was neglected when locked up in a camp in Texas. Then she comes to Topaz camp during that mean winter. It was not fair. I prayed for her to get better. I had wished so much that she would again help the teachers as she had in Topaz camp. She is so smart and kind and knows so many things she has not even told me yet. It was so nice to be near her like when we studied at home in San Francisco.

Then a strange thing happened. Just after I thought about Grandma, I found a little carved Buddha in front of a nearby apartment. Looking around to see if anyone was close, and finding no one, I sat down next to it.

Whispering I asked, "Oh Lord Buddha, please help me and don't be mad because we don't do meditation much. We are in much trouble. Our Grandma is very sick and has had a hard time getting well. She is so good and kind, we love her so. She has never done anything bad or wrong, even though the FBI took her away. Please watch over her so she can stay with us forever, please. My name is Miyako, but I'm called Kitty, thank you."

I could feel someone standing near me. I got startled trying to look up at him, but the sun was in my eyes. I fell back and sort of cried.

"Please little one, I'm very sorry if I scared you. I could see you were praying. That is good. Here we all are in much need of that, especially now."

All I could do was squint and stare up at him, shading my eyes from the sun, I asked, "Is this your Buddha? Is it OK I be here?"

"Yes, but he belongs really to no one, just everybody, that is the way. Buddha is anyone's. My name is Toah, that is what they call me, and who might you be?"

"I'm Kitty, well, that is just what I am called, my name is Miyako."

"Oh, yes, a very sacred name, you were born to happiness, but you seem so sad."

"It's my Grandma, she is ill, she is in the little hospital. I was asking Lord Buddha for some help for her, we miss her, my family." I now had another friend, Mr. Toah Izawa, much like Mr. Omori whom I had met in Tanforan.

"Do you know Mr. Omori? I hope he is here. There are so many people, and I hope to see him again."

"Well, no, but I will try to help. Don't you have any friends your age?"

"Not many, we just got here from Topaz camp. We keep moving and I really want to go home now. It seems like just when school and other things start getting good, we move. But I am going to have my favorite teacher now. Still, I want to go home now anyway."

"Where is your home Kitty?"

"San Francisco, and we have a nice little garden. And there is a really big park in the City and a really great big bridge, the Golden Gate. Where is your home?" I asked.

"Well, I'm from Honolulu, before that, Hiroshima."

"Oh wow, I am from Hawai'i, Hilo. Are others from Hawai'i here?"

"Yes, there are many, maybe your family knows some of them. I will find out. And they should like to meet my new friend, a nice little Buddha head."

"What, what you call me?"

"Oh, that is quite a compliment. How have you not heard that before being from Hawai'i?"

I just laughed, "I was only just over three when I left Hawai'i and came to San Francisco. But that's OK, gotta tell my sister, she would know dakine you say. Please can you tell me, what do the words, disloyal and loyal mean?"

"Well Kitty, I think I know what you are asking. You see, some people who run the camps are convinced that many, if not all of us, are not loyal to America. This is because we adults have not answered their strange questions, or behaved exactly like they wanted or expected us to. Also, too many in the government are very prejudiced. It's now a great misunderstanding which brings everyone grief and trouble."

Later I found other kids in the fields picking up shells.

"May I do that too?"

"Sure," one boy said, "and there are some arrow heads the Indians left from a long time ago."

Was this an Indian camp? Were they locked up like us? I wondered to myself.

One older boy explained that thousands of years ago there had been an ancient inland sea or lake in what is now Tule Lake. Named after the Tule grasses growing in the lakes. It is also home to migratory birds.

I could see that most of the kids had already gathered the good, not broken, shells so I decided to collect only those that were partly broken. I still felt funny, and did not want to invade what they were already doing. I was still shy and afraid. I really wanted some friends, not knowing always what to say to others. It was hard.

I heard some people speaking Japanese. Would I not be liked because I could not speak Japanese? It felt like that before, in Tanforan, when I was confused and afraid that I might not know what to do or say. All those things still bothered me. I had been trying to learn Japanese words, but that was hard.

Then I was suddenly in our little garden at home. Where I could play and dance and not feel everyone was watching. It was warm and nice. There was the music I missed. It made me happy and there was nothing to be afraid of, I felt better.

"Why does Kitty sometimes just sit and stare? I don't think she is looking at anything," I heard Tomiko ask Mom.

"I guess she is in a day dream. I think it's OK."

I was very happy and it was good to start school again. At Topaz camp the teacher suggested that I might be able to study to skip a grade. She explained that I would be starting a new school year in the fall and would not have to attend the last of the other school year if I studied enough to skip that half year, so I could instead begin the fourth grade in the Fall if I qualified, by studying and passing the tests.

My teacher, Miss Hart, gave me all the subjects and the

studies I needed if I was to catch up to the fourth grade and still do the third grade studies as well. I didn't know if I could. I was afraid I might not be able to do all that stuff. Then I thought of what Grandma said. Everyone was counting on me. I was scared and thought about talking to the little Buddha.

After some of my first studies Mom sent me on an errand for Dad. It gave me a chance to look around more for my friends. That day when coming home, I met Yuke for the first time since Tanforan. She had been in Topaz, but very far from where we lived. She had been very sick with pneumonia at Topaz, and only got better during the summer. She had lost some of her school grade, so she was a little behind. We had lots to talk over. I was so happy to see her.

Mom and Tomiko got jobs at the mess. Michio entered his junior classes and like Eichi, found a teacher who answered questions about civil rights and history. He wanted to keep up with his brother who might soon be in Europe or North Africa with the army.

In October, one of the camp trucks carrying workers on a nearby farm turned over. One man was killed. A committee of camp representatives, the *Daihyo Sha Kai,* wanted to have a funeral. The camp director denied them out of hand. But just like at Topaz, a funeral was held. It was nice, a Buddhist priest presided, but it was very sad. Dad attended one of the committees where it was decided to talk to the camp director about instituting better safety regulations and improved working conditions.

"The camp director has refused to negotiate or to recognize the committee," Dad said. "There is going to be a work stoppage, there could be a strike," he said.

A few weeks later Dad gave us some serious news. There was a work stoppage and again the camp director would not talk to the committee, so they called a strike. The director fired all of the workers and had workers from Poston and Topaz camps harvest the crops around the Tule Lake camp community.

"The strike breakers are going to earn an extra one dollar an hour. That means in two days they will get what our workers made in a week," Dad reported.

In school there was a lot of talk about the firing of those who worked in the fields. "Now my Dad does not have a job," one of my classmates, David, said. "We could have used the money."

I heard the neighbors complaining about inmates from other camps harvesting the local crops.

"That was the cruelest trick ever. Using some internees against other internees," Dad said. "But we are powerless. It's hopeless."

I could see that Dad was really discouraged. "That is why some are giving up and want to even renounce their citizenship as is now being suggested by some militants. It's hard to fight that director and the WRA," he said.

After three weeks of study of the fourth grade and third grade school work, Miss Hart started giving me some tests.

I was scared. There was so much to keep remembering. After I passed some studies a different teacher gave me more tests. She sat with me and asked me questions. That was really hard. She did not tell me how I did. That worried me. I was then given more subjects to study and Miss Hart again gave me more tests. I was getting tired of all the tests and wanted to quit, but they would not let me quit.

On the weekends I was happy to visit Grandma.

"How are you doing Kitty?" Grandma asked.

"I keep getting tested on subjects that I'm not even sure I studied enough. It is not easy and I am getting tired," I answered. "There is so much to know. Some are tests where I have to write or chose the right answer. Or a teacher asks a question and I answer it. A problem or some name or date. Those are the hardest. Having to figure out something. I hope I am pau soon."

"Well, it sounds like you are doing well. You just told me a lot. Now I must rest again. Tell everybody hello and love and to visit, I miss them."

"Thank you Grandma, I love you. Good night."

In the middle of the next week, I had to take another test. A week later I had to meet with both teachers. They seemed very serious and talked to each other while I waited. I was now very scared and jittery. Then Miss Hart asked me to stand. I shook and got really scared.

"Kitty, I would like to congratulate you. You are now a fourth grader," she said. I cried.

"You mean I skipped half a semester?"

"Yes, the school superintendent has given final approval."

I didn't understand what that exactly meant, but was happy I did not have to take any more tests for a long while. I could almost not wait until I was able to visit Grandma.

"Oh, *Sobosan,* Grandma, guess what happened? I'm in the fourth grade and you were right. I practiced and studied and passed all the tests. So I'm experienced. What do you think?"

Grandma could hardly talk, but she had lots of smiles.

"Oh please, you gotta get better," I had happy tears and sadness. I stayed later that day until Grandma said it was best I not miss supper and school, as I could visit another day.

I was so worried and stopped by the little Buddha, whispering, "Oh please Lord Buddha, Grandma is still sick. I hope she will get better. I will visit her as much as I can. She helped me with my studies. And I got success. I love her so. Please help her. Thank you, this is Kitty speaking."

Each free time after school, I hurried until I got to the hospital. I was sometimes out of breath by the time I arrived to visit Grandma. On weekends, after doing my studies, and chores, I visited her.

On one visit while I was reading to Grandma I noticed she was sleeping. It was nearly time for dinner, so I went to the hospital kitchen. They had allowed me to bring Grandma her dinner. When I was sick with measles she had stayed with me and made my meals.

When I returned with the meal tray she was still sleeping. So I waited. Everything was very still and quiet. Grandma looked so beautiful and peaceful. I was hoping that at last she would be getting better. Food for the other patients was arriving and then someone said, "Kitty, it's best you wake up your Grandmother before her meal gets cold."

I leaned near and spoke very softly, "Grandma, it's time to eat now…wake up Grandma, please wake now, your food is here."

Then I asked a nurse, "My Grandma is still sleeping, what can I do? Can you wake her please? I don't want to bother the other patients. Thank you."

But the nurse did something strange, she picked me up and told another nurse to take me from the room.

"No, it is OK I be here." Frightened and confused, I pushed the nurse from me.

"No, I want my Grandma, I want *Sobosan*, my Grandma." I was bewildered and started crying. "Please, I just want to be here with my Grandma. Why can't I stay? I do no wrong. What is going on?"

Someone told another person to call my parents. I was scared, crying and shaking. I could feel my heart thumping. Everything was confusing.

"What did I do? What is wrong? Please let me go to Grandma, please."

The nurse kneeled down and hugged me, she also was crying a little. I was awfully confused and crying a whole lot.

"Kitty, your grandmother is happy now. She is no longer sick. She is with God. See? She is smiling."

The nurse took me over and I looked at Grandma and I think I reached out and touched her shoulder. I just looked at her for the longest time. Crying, I must have put my head on her pillow. I tried to reach out and hold her hand.

I think that something happened. Maybe I fell, or things were falling. I could not understand. Things just got blurry and there were lots of sounds all around. It was very confusing and then there was a funny quiet, like in a dream. But I did not want to be dreaming. I just wanted Grandma.

I thought I saw Tomiko, Mom and Dad, Michio and then Eichi. I knew Eichi was far away, but I wanted to ask my big brother for help. I kept asking for Grandma. There were lots of people talking, but I could not understand them. I spoke, but no one heard me. I said that I was sorry.

Then it felt like I was floating. I kept calling for Grandma. I was running home. I kept running, but could not seem to get home. Music was playing. I was sitting in our little garden and crying. I kept telling everybody that I did not want to sleep. It was very quiet and some kids were looking at me. I started to run again.

After a while, I saw Grandma. She was in the garden, but I just kept looking and crying and saying that I did not want to sleep. I could hear someone calling me.

"No, no," I kept saying, "not now." Then I was alone and nowhere. I was so lonely. I wanted to be home.

It seemed like a long time, then I felt happy and it seemed a little like being home. I opened my eyes and looked around, but I knew I was in camp, in the apartment.

I shut my eyes. I heard Tomiko whisper, "Kitty, Kitty, wake up now. You have to eat. Here, here's some miso, careful, it's still hot."

"Where? What? Oh, is it time for school?" I asked.

"No, not today, you have been sleeping for a long time. We were all so worried."

I kept to myself the rest of that day. It was kind of strange and hard to remember where I had been. Then I did not want to remember anything.

"I gave her something to eat earlier," Tomiko said to Mom.

"Kitty, do you want to go have supper?" Mom asked.

I went to supper with everyone. Everyone hugged me and asked how I was feeling.

"I'm OK," I said. But I didn't know how to answer much. We all ate dinner together. Mom was happy because we were all sitting at one table. It seemed nice and I was smiling and feeling happy.

I was not sure what was going on. I knew Grandma was gone. But I just couldn't remember. So I went back to school. Everyone at home was nice to me and did not ask any questions. No one in school said anything, and they were very nice to me. Fourth grade didn't seem much different from third grade.

I visited the little Buddha and sat, but I didn't know what to say. Then again on another day, I don't know why, I just whispered, "Oh thank you Lord Buddha for my Grandma. I know she is happy and does not have any sickness, but I am missing her. She is so wise. I did not get to learn all she knew. I am so very sorry. Please help me to learn more that she knew. I loved her and miss her so much. She kept telling me to study and learn. I promise to keep studying and learning. Someday maybe I will know as much as she knew. I will try very hard, honest."

Sleep sometimes came, but waking was not always fun. Sometimes, when I thought too much, I did not want to remember anything. When I cried often, I tried not to let anyone see me. When I thought about Grandma I wondered what could I have done to help her. I wanted to talk to someone, but I thought maybe I shouldn't. Everyone was so busy. I thought Lord Buddha might get tired of me talking to him and always asking for help.

One day, I saw Dr. Namamura. I was so surprised and happy.

"Doctor, hi, how are you and your wife doing?" He turned when he saw and heard me and smiled and held out his arms to me.

"My, what a surprise, one of my favorite patients. But what are you doing in this camp?"

"My family could not stay in Topaz. It was those questions, the loyalty problems. Is that why you are here?" I asked.

"Oh yes, such a problem. We are also victims of the nightmare. But let's talk about pleasant things. How are you doing? Have you found many shells and those little arrowheads?"

"Just a few broken arrowheads. I miss reading your books. Do you still have the medical ones? I don't really understand them, but I still like them."

We went to his apartment and his wife gave us some tea and we talked about medicine and doctors. He wanted to know if I wanted to study medicine some day when I had more school. I told him I was not sure, but that I liked to read about medicine and doctors. He gave me another book to borrow and said that I should write down questions. He would try to answer them when I visited again.

"I am happy you are keeping cleaner. Congratulations," he said.

About a month after Grandma left us, I asked Mom and Dad, "What happens to Grandma? I miss her. I don't remember much," I said.

They explained that she had been taken to a mortuary in Oregon and maybe, like Grandpa, we can take her when we can go home.

"You mean we can go home with her to San Francisco soon? I asked.

Mom hugged me and said that she hoped we could still go home. What she said made me feel happier.

At school the kids talked about the camp. The "no-nos." It was hard to study sometimes when they were arguing, in class or after.

I heard a man I knew from Topaz camp talking about renouncing. I told Dad when he came home.

"Remember the man in Topaz camp who was mad at you about Eichi going in the army? He is speaking to everyone about renouncing their citizenship and going to Japan. It scares me. What we going to do? Grandma said you would not. Lots of my friends are worried too, and don't want to go to Japan," I said.

"Oh Kitty, please avoid him. He is part of a growing group of militant "no-nos". They are recruiting others, including citizens to renounce and accompany them to Japan. Like us, they transferred here. But their intentions are different from ours. They consider us to be "loyalists" because we do not intend to renounce our citizenship and follow their agenda.

Hopefully they will leave us alone. Many of them are our neighbors, and like some of us, they answered "no-no" to those damn questionnaires. Just like us, they have been betrayed by America, but have chosen to give up and return to Japan. The Issei among them and the Nisei are renouncing their citizenship and so will be deported to Japan," he answered.

In early November, we heard that the big WRA director from Washington, D.C. was visiting our camp.

"The *Daihyo Sha Kai* requested a meeting with him and the camp director. The negotiation committee wants to give them a list of all the inmate grievances," Dad said.

A few days later, the block chairman told us that the camp director would not take the list of grievances or meet with the committee. Then we heard that there was a group of inmates who gathered to protest when some of the warehouse food supplies were being taken from Tule Lake camp to a nearby former civilian conservation corps camp for feeding the strikebreakers. The strikebreakers had been performing work of the camp workers previously fired who had attempted to protest working conditions conducted by the camp administration. The strikebreakers had been imported by the WRA from other concentration camps.

"The camp security seized our friends who were protesting. We hear that a number of them were beaten and thrown in the stockade," Dad said.

"What is a stockade?" I asked.

He explained that the camp administration had set up an area near to the jail, which became the stockade.

Dad said it seems to be like a temporary jail for those who are protesting, but the inmates are held without being charged.

A week later, I went with Dad to pick up the family's mail. There were many inmates near the camp administration. Dad said they were protesting about the treatment of the fired workers who had complained about wages, lost jobs and food shortages. Dad said that they had come to discuss matters with the camp administrator and then he left me to go with them while I waited with others for the mail.

Suddenly, there were big bangs and smoke that startled all of us waiting for the mail. Smoke was everywhere. I ran toward the hospital. Smoke was stinging my eyes and I could not find the doorway. Then someone picked me up and took me inside the hospital. Some were trying to leave. I still could not see, the smoke hurt and I was crying when someone stopped me and put a soft wet rag in my face and hugged me. I looked up and saw a nurse I knew.

"There, there, just relax, you will be all right. Kitty, isn't it? Do you remember me? You used to visit. I'm Trina."

"Is it war now?" I asked. "I don't like it, what we gonna do? I am afraid."

"No, not that, not war, at least not here. I'm not sure what is going on, but you better wait here for a while until things quiet down. Hold still, I'm washing your eyes out so they will stop stinging. It's from the tear gas. I don't understand either. Best you stay with the others. It's not safe out there."

After a while, I slowly went outside to see if I could see Dad. It was still hard to see. Then I saw him with other protesters. The smoke had starting going away. So I left the hospital to go to where he was standing. But then some security police and soldiers were taking Dad and the others through one of the gates. Soldiers and police were moving toward all of us.

They were big and scary and I didn't know what to do. Seeing Dad, I started running between the soldiers and police yelling for him until I reached to the gate. It was locked and I bumped into it kind of hard. It hurt, so I began hitting and kicking it. I saw Dad and others going away. I tried yelling for him, "Daddy! Daddy!" But he was too far away to hear me.

I didn't really know why I ran, but no one stopped me or did anything to me. I was all by myself, I was mad, and kept hitting the gate. Then I turned around and noticed the soldiers standing behind me very still, looking down at me. They were so big, I wanted to hit them, but I was afraid. So I started running between them toward the barracks. No one stopped me and I did not look back and I did not know why I did all that.

Maybe they did not stop me because I was so little and they were so big? I don't know. I could have been in lots of trouble. Just like some other times, no one paid attention to me. That seemed OK, because I was really very frightened, but mad about Dad being taken away.

What happened to Dad was unfair. He would not be able to work his co-op job and we needed the money. I knew he did nothing wrong.

Later, the block chairman told us the military, the police and the administration had misunderstood the crowd of protesters and feared they were rioting. The arrested protesters, including Dad, were kept in the stockade without any formal processes.

A little later, on the 14th of November, martial law was declared. The Army had taken over the camp. Many camp operations came to a stop, except the mess halls, the hospital and our schools. Then finally on January 15th, 1944, martial law had been withdrawn.

On the day that Dad got arrested, when I got home, Mom asked, "Where is your father? He was supposed to be with you,"

I began to cry, "He got gassed, everybody, and me too. Lots of people running, and smoke all over the place, the army was attacking everyone. I'm sorry he got locked up with others. I didn't mean to lose him. Oh please, honest, I am very sorry," I told her.

When all of us wanted to find out what happened to those taken, including our Dad, we got yelled at and told to go back to the barracks.

I sort of had a birthday party that December, my eighth, but now with Grandmother gone and Dad in the stockade and my biggest brother away, there was just Mom, Tomiko, Michio, and me. I asked myself, how old will I be before we get out of some darn camp?

"This martial law is so hard. Food is getting scarce. Milk and tea are gone and rice is very scarce. There is hardly enough rice for mocha for the New Year," Mom said.

After New Year's day it started getting colder. The coal deliveries were delayed and hot water was cutoff for days at a time. Running water was off for part of some days.

Everyone in camp was under curfew from six to six. They had daily searches for, they said, "contraband," but I never figured out what they were looking for. The army guys just barged in our apartment, and went through our stuff. Other times they were looking for committee members, called. The *Daiho Sha Kai* who had not been arrested and put in the stockade like Dad, but were hid by internees. If they were found, they were sent to the stockade and some held for months without any hearing or trial.

Some committee members who were still hiding later gave up and turned themselves in. I heard that they did not like the army harassing everyone during the searches.

I decided not to say the Pledge of Allegiance when it was my turn in our school class.

"I can't for now, I really don't understand how come we are free and locked up. And now dis martial law stuff."

Miss Hart was not happy and said only, "thank you, Kitty for your honesty."

Around Christmas, the Red Cross came to give gifts and

food for each family. They said they were sorry for not having more due to the war. The school class wrote a "thank you" and gave some money that we collected.

When the New Year came, things were very quiet. Not many cared since we were "under siege," Mom called it. But some older inmates did tell everyone, "*Shinned omedeto gozai masu*" – Happy New Year, a new saying I had learned from before in Topaz camp.

After nearly four weeks, Dad and some other inmates returned, but some leaders stayed in the stockade. Dad did not explain and said little about what happened, except that he was angry and did not want to talk any more about what happened.

"Dad, we really missed you!" I cried out, running to hug him.

"Can't we do anything? We didn't even get to find out why they locked you guys up. I asked. Can't we do something about all that happened?" Mom asked.

"There is nothing we can do, probably ever. That's the reason we are in a concentration camp. We have no freedoms here. We can only just be careful and hope things will not get worse. I'm sorry to say, it's hard on everyone," Dad said.

We learned from the block committee that during martial law, food and other supplies were stolen and sold by administration employees to the local black-market.

"Meals are being reduced for inmates, but not for the camp

employees," Dad said. "We cannot get any answers from the camp director. Everyone is keeping quiet. There is a great fear by everyone of being punished for complaining or protesting. We suspect that those who stole food and other supplies had to be some camp employees, soldiers or both because we were all locked up at the time. They had attempted to blame some of us before when there were questions of theft from the warehouse."

Arrests continued for others implicated in the strikes and other protests. With the arrests and releases there was a continuing turnover of inmates forced to live in the stockade, which housed approximately 200 persons on a daily average.

I thought we were lucky after the first of the year when only once did a soldier search our apartment. Then we heard knocking on the apartment next door. "Everyone stay still, don't look out the window or open the door," Mom said.

Tomiko and I kept still together in my bed. Listening, we could hear people questioning our neighbor. It was not hard to hear the rough voices of the soldiers.

"They are intimidating that poor family," Mom said.

All the time we just prayed that they would not come to question us. Dad had gone out earlier to secretly meet with others who were planning appeals for help from the Spanish embassy. Spain was neutral, they had been mediating talks between the U.S. and Japan for Issei inmates who had appealed and protested their treatment by the WRA.

Japan, we heard, had protested the United States' treatment of all persons of Japanese descent/ancestry, during the war.

When martial law was lifted, things calmed down. Some of our neighbors were allowed to work in the fields and at jobs in the camp. We were happy that Dad got to go back to work so we could get some food we needed.

One day at school I learned some strange news and told Dad, "My friend David's dad said that there are German POWs working with him cutting alfalfa who came to work without any soldiers escorting or guarding them. He has also learned that their POW camp is not far from here. It is very nice, and different from the way we live."

"Thank you Kitty, I will have to find out if that is true or just a rumor," he replied.

Several weeks later, Dad and several neighbors verified the information on the POWs. They discovered that the German POWs were housed two to four workers each in furnished living quarters with indoor plumbing, heating and eating facilities. A small contingent of soldiers did guard their camp, but the German POW workers were often unescorted to and from their assigned work areas in the local communities around Tule Lake camp. Another neighbor who became acquainted with the POWs was told that locals in the greater community often invited the Germans to their homes for dinner and other social activities.

About that same time, some of my school classmates were talking about seeing POWs walking near the camp.

"We were near the fence on the east side of the camp when four of the POW guys waved at us. They didn't answer when we told them they were "damn Germans" and there were no soldiers with them like when our parents sometimes get to work outside the camp," a classmate said.

Everyone in Tule Lake camp knew that no one in the camp was ever allowed to get friendly with locals in the community. It had already been known that locals were very hostile toward us. It made us kids mad because we had brothers and dads in the war fighting those Germans and Italians.

When Dad and other inmates went to meet with the camp administration with the information, they were badly threatened and told that such allegations were not true and could lead to harsh consequences if such issues were raised or pursued.

"When some of us attempted to insist on an investigation the camp administrator had the security personnel physically escort us from the building. One of the men and his wife were both pushed and she fell down and had to go to the hospital to have a doctor look at her. Fortunately she was OK," Dad said.

"Security men were waving their night sticks at us and ordering us away from the director's office and the administration building. It was disgusting and demoralizing to realize that my son and others in Europe were fighting a war against those two countries and here there were soldiers of those two countries free to go and come freely in this country, while we citizens were locked up and treated like the aliens. They are the real enemy, not us," he said.

Tomiko was able to get a housekeeping job. It was in the home of one of the camp's administration employees. They were a Quaker family, The Hendersons. The husband was a contentious objector who was assigned to the camp as his punishment for being a pacifist. On a few occasions during the weekends, Tomiko was able to take me with her to help with the work and babysitting. They had two beautiful children, one three and one about one year old. They were very sympathetic to our being locked up. I think that is the right word. But we had to keep the pay to ourselves. Wages were controlled by the camp administration and ours were less than those wages given to outside civilians in the community.

After a week we could no longer work there. "But Mom, why can't me an Tomiko keep working for the Henderson's? They are a nice family, and we need the money. They don't hate us like some other people out there in the community," I told her.

"Because you and your sister are receiving less wages than our neighbors, and if someone from outside the camp performed the same work. That is unfair to you two, or other neighbors working for camp employees," Mom said.

Later, the Henderson's paid us from their own money. But when word reached the camp administration, the practice was halted and they were reprimanded, almost losing their jobs with the camp administration.

After martial law ended in mid-January 1944, there was never again any real trust between the inmates and the camp administrators. It seemed like we all feared them. And we even feared talking with each other in case the wrong person was listening.

I liked to listen to one neighbor's radio when they played classical music. Just after we were all under martial law, the news reported that there were riots at Tule Camp.

"Dad, the news on the radio says there has been insurrection and riots here," I told him.

He laughed. "Look at this newspaper. I didn't want to show your mother, she seems upset enough."

It was a local newspaper that had reported the same thing I heard, and that there were armed gangs in the camp. It said that they were being "bravely put down by the army."

When I took the newspaper to class for others to read, some kids went around looking for the rioters who were being bravely put down by the army but we never found them.

The army had not come into the camp. We knew there were no inmates rioting or being put down. We all laughed and made jokes about the army and the news stories that were not true.

At school another day, Rika said, "My mom heard on the radio that some more of the people living near the camp are complaining that all of us are being coddled and having leisure time while they work to feed us," she said.

"We know it is not true, but I don't know what we can do about it," I said. "It just hurts us and makes us look so bad, that is unfair."

What was also unfair was that our teachers could not discuss those rumors and talk of the news reports with us.

Some of the class decided to write a letter to a local newspaper about the news reports not being true. But the school superintendent refused to send it to the newspaper. He visited the classes and warned the students that if any are talking about news reports, they will be disciplined. He said that each of us should report to our teacher any students reading or talking about the news. He said we were not supposed to be reading any outside newspapers. That we could be punished if we were caught with them. One of our neighbors said that camp militants who called themselves Kachigum, meaning "victory group," kept saying that Japan was winning the war, and that was one reason they wanted to segregate them from "loyalists" in the camp.

"Dad, can you explain why some want to segregate from the rest of us in the camp? I am confused who they are. Some say they are the militants," I asked.

"Your question has two parts that the WRA created," Dad said. "The first part: The WRA decided that those of us from all the concentration camps who they said were "disloyal" were transferred here. The Tule Lake Relocation Center became the Tule Lake Segregation Center. Then those who the WRA said were loyal were transferred to those camps we left, except for a number of internees here who the WRA said were loyal, but refused to be transferred elsewhere. The second part has to do with a number of internees who lost faith in the system since the beginning of the internment. It was especially Issei and Kibei and some Nisei who were distressed over their mistreatment by America.

Both Issei and Kibei (Kibei are Nisei youth educated in Japan) had good reason to believe that they had little alternative but to turn to Japan rather than continue to tolerate the mistreatment here. They concluded that they had no future.

They formed into groups, the *Hokoou-Hoshidan* and their elders, the *Saikakuri Keigan.* Their common agenda was to re-segregate themselves from the remaining camp inmates who they called "loyalists," that's us."

"So they want to separate from us and then go to Japan?" I said.

"Yes, that is right, Kitty. Whereas all we generally want to do is continue to bide our time as best we can and then return to our homes and lives here in America. Now, hopefully we will be able to co-exist with that group. But their agenda is very militant and some of their beliefs are very strong and sincere. They therefore want to convince all Nisei to renounce and return with them. Some of the group have referred to loyalists as "inu"(dogs) for opposing their agenda, or just wishing to be neutral. Some even suspect that many of us are cooperating with the camp administration, which is untrue. We are caught between the militant group and the camp administration."

"Some of those militants keep saying that Japan is winning the war," I said.

"Just ignore them," Dad said. "I don't know where they are getting their news. And I doubt many neighbors believe them."

About a week later, I learned that a lot of my classmates wanted to leave classes early because they were going to Japanese classes to study their culture and language. I ran to my parents.

"Mom, Dad, some students want to be excused from school early to go to the militants' school. Others are confused and scared, they don't want to go to the militants' school for fear that they will have to go to Japan," I said.

"Don't worry, Kitty," Mom said, "we are arranging meetings with their teachers to negotiate a sharing of times so no one going to the regular school will lose credits. And, all students who wish, can take advantage of Japanese language and culture classes. They are our neighbors and though there might be some differences, their intentions are well meaning. The students should not be afraid. Taking the militants' classes does not mean they would then have to go to Japan," Mom said.

I understood and thought it good that there was a chance to learn some more Japanese language. Both Tomiko and I were excited to learn some of the culture too. Michio said he was going to find out about flower arranging, and other classes.

We knew the militant's goal was to leave camp and be

deported to Japan. But our family did not like it that they were always trying to persuade Nisei families to renounce their citizenship.

"We all are under a great deal of pressure, and in some cases intimated, for not renouncing," Mom and Dad said.

"I don't believe they should pressure anyone to renounce. Citizenship is so precious. It is no time to make a hasty decision you might regret," Michio said.

Our family could see that the group was very small, and was not known to the camp administration, but within a few weeks it started growing. Both Mom and Dad talked about it. I knew they were worried.

Dad said, "The camp administration does not realize that the militant group is expanding over most of the camp. Those in the administration are failing to notice, and I think I know why. Having crushed some of us with their fascist tactics they have become complacent. The same attitude they had when we were initially locked up. It will suddenly become apparent to them, too soon, and the rest of us will suffer."

"Many of our neighbors in the blocks and others have renounced," Dad reported. "They were intimidated into renouncing."

"Do you think it was because the militant groups were just small at the beginning?" Tomiko asked.

"That is right, you are catching on. It was at first seen that the group's intentions were merely to offer their language and cultural activities as positive actions for our community. Their real intent, however, was to get more people to renounce their U.S. citizenship," Dad said.

"So the camp administration essentially ignored the militants' real intentions," Michio said.

"Yes," Dad answered. "They have abandoned their responsibilities and allowed the remainder of the camp to be intimidated and abused at the hands of a minority intent on renunciation of the citizenship of all Nisei."

"It has been disappointing," Mom said. "We have worked with the militants' programs, but there is some conflict with the regular camp routine. Such as school, recreation and other activities. They want to change our programs to meet their nationalistic (Japanese) goals to prepare internees to return to Japan," she concluded.

"But Mom, what can we do? Now the camp administration people are not doing anything," I said. "We are not going to Japan. But a lot of my friends are worried. They don't know if they want to continue with the language and culture classes. Some fear that their parents may renounce."

Then Michio announced. "The radio says that the Congress just passed a law allowing Nisei to renounce their citizenship and it was just signed by the president, FDR."

"Isn't that what the militants wanted to happen?" Tomiko asked.

"Yes," Dad said. "The Congress and FDR, are under the influence and pressures of the nativist and jingoistic groups in America. Consequently they have played into the militants' intent that we all renounce and go to Japan with them," he said. I believe that the WRA has unknowingly accomplished the intent of various racist elements in America who succeeded in having us interned, to also deprive us our citizenship," he concluded.

"That is all so depressing. But I just don't believe our citizenship can simply be voted away by ignorant bigoted congressmen" Mom said. "Why doesn't the president realize what is going on?"

"Maybe he does not give a damn," Michio said. Militants and others would arise at 5:30 a.m. each morning to the sound of buglers, and sing the *Kimigayo* (Japanese national anthem) which spoke of freedom and peace. They also performed calisthenics. Many men wore their heads shaven, with headbands (bozo) and marched to the cadence of calls of,"*Washo-sho! Washo-sho!*"Participating women wore long skirts and their hair in braids.

Tomiko and I found it interesting and funny since both of us wore our hair in braids.

"I like to wear a bozo, they look neat, my hair has not yet grown much since I got out of the stockade," Michio said.

Rumors continued to add to the family's concerns. There were also many more false stories of victories by Japanese forces in the Pacific.

"I also saw a newspaper that reported harassment and beatings of former inmates. Families who had been released early from the camps," Mom said.

The militants, having heard the same news told everybody, "See, no one can return to their homes, we must continue to renounce and go to Japan, we are not wanted here."

Some militants spoke at the mess during evening meal. They interrupted our peace and upset us I felt. I tried to speak out then, but they seemed to ignore me. That is when Dad warned everybody, our family and others, not to talk openly about our opposition to the renunciation of citizenship.

He was right. A lot of the militants were very scary and angry sometimes. I knew they were still our friends and neighbors. It was so difficult to worry about doing something that someone might not like that would cause them to hurt us. Like Mom and Dad, I kept hoping, that we could just wait out our time and go to our home in San Francisco.

The soldiers and administration security police frightened me more than the militants. If I went out of the apartment and saw the soldiers, police or some militants I would go somewhere else or go back another way when I saw one or more coming into our block. How could they ever think we would give them any respect when they were so mean and hurtful?

From what some friendly militants said to us I could imagine how the Issei men and women might dream of being in their home country, Japan. There they would be welcomed. In America, there was only racism and uncertainty. It was a shame that for all of the years that they worked hard, raised families had loved the land, they were only to be discarded, locked up and treated as less than human. I had really thought hard about all that, and I wanted them to stop hurting our Issei.

In the late fall of 1944 we were all notified by the WRC that most of the camps would be closed in a year. There was no information on Tule Lake. They said it was because of a U.S. Supreme Court decision where the Court said that it had been illegal to retain citizens and that the internment of Nissei, citizens was in violation of the due process of the Constitution.

"The news of the decision," Dad said, "had been purposely and politically delayed by FDR until after his reelection early in November."

I asked my teacher, when she told us about the Supreme Court Decision. "How come the president could stop that news until after his re-election? Was he supposed to do that?" I asked.

She did not answer and started talking about something else. Then I remember what Dad had told me about how teachers are sometimes not allowed to discuss sensitive issues.

It sure was sensitive. When I got home Mom was in a terrible mood. She hardly ever was really mad.

"After all this time, they had no right what-so-ever to lock us up!" Mom screamed at Dad. "Why did they (JACL) go along with the evacuation if it was illegal? Why did you listen and support them? Why didn't you oppose them when they told us it was necessary for us to cooperate? It was not necessary. All these long years we have suffered. Oh why? Why? After all this time and everything!"

I had never heard her like that. She was shaking her head at Dad. I just stayed still. He did not answer her, but walked out of the apartment. She started crying.

I didn't know what to do. I was so scared and left and met Tomiko who was just outside the door.

"What are we gonna do?" I asked her.
"I don't know, but we should not say anything for now."

We hugged and cried.

Michio, Tomiko and me stayed close, but did not say anything about what happened. I did not wish to go to school or stay home. There were few places that did not remind me of the apartment and everything. We all knew how Mom felt. That was the way we felt too. I felt sad for Dad. I wanted to run away.

"Will we ever get happy again? Why can't we all go home now, right now? We not havta be locked up, then why was it all done?" I asked Tomiko. She just shook her head.

I visited the little Buddha and sat quietly with him. Then I got up and wandered until I got to a camp fence. I felt sick. Mom and Dad had never really got so mad before. Leaning on the fence I hit and kicked it until I got I tired and sat against it crying.

Then I was standing in a corner of my old school yard, a group of kids were pointing at me and yelling that name again. Scared, I ran into a hallway, down some stairs and out into the yard. I wanted to hide, but I could not. Those kids kept chasing and yelling things I wanted to forget. I fell as they were throwing rocks at me.

I yelled, "Oh please you guys stop it I did nothing wrong, why are you doing this?"

Suddenly I awoke up and David, my good friend was looking down at me and smiling.

"Hey you been sleepin, come on wake up! Kitty, it's me," he said dropping little shells and pebbles on me. I felt happy to still be in camp.

"Gee, sorry, I musta scared you, you was sleeping and making all kind of noise and talking to yourself so I woke you."

"Oh, hi, yeah, dreamin bad."

"What were you dreaming?"

"Jes bad stuff. I wanna go home. We not belong here, never, ever."

"Yeah, you are right, but nothing we can do."

"Well for now let's run away, go someplace, but first I wanna climb that tower," I said pointing to one nearby.

"But there are guards in them an they got guns. We could get in trouble," David said.

"Yeah, I know. It is kinda scary and exciting and it is there," I said.

David did not say anything more. We went over to the fences and started squeezing under each of them. It was really easy. When I got to the tower ladder he gave me a boost so I could reach the rungs. He followed me. It was so easy and fun. I looked down and started to get dizzy.

"Don't look down," I said. "Let's just keep going up."

"Oh it's nice, I can see a lot of the camp and some fields," David said.

I know I was getting us into trouble. But it seemed to be fun and we were going to be brave. It was exciting.

"Oh wow, oh boy, this is neat, I can see way over to all the rail road tracks and other farms where the animals are kept, it is really nice," I said.

"Yeah, an look at the people, they sure look funny, so little. I wish we had a spy glass so we could see even more things," David said.

"Oh, we had one, but the FBI men took it away from us," I replied.

"Why? Did they need it in the war?"

"Well yeah, I guess. They take stuff from you guys too?"

"I think just a radio my Dad used to hear farm reports, but it didn't matter, because they also took him away. My mom, sister an me had to live in town until we went to the fairgrounds, and then to camp." David said.

It was really fun looking over the camp from so high. There was so much to see. We seemed to be on top of everything and felt really good and different. But then we heard screams from way down in the camp yard below us.

It kinda frightened us. Neighbors were yelling and pointing at us and others were running toward the fence and the tower. Above us we heard someone walking around, but we could not see who. We kept quiet and still. It was a tower guard. I think he was saying something to himself or maybe about us or to us.

"Oh darn, what we gonna do now? I don't think I can go down, I'm kinda dizzy," David whispered.

"You be OK, jes keep climbing up here," I answered.

I had reached the catwalk and helped David. When we stood up we could see the tower guard. He stared at us With his mouth open and making a bad face, but he did not say anything. He was opposite us on the other side of the tower catwalk.

"Hey, what the hell? You two halt! Come here at once!" he yelled.

I looked at David, "how do we do that, halt?"

"I don't know," David said.

Then the guard began running on the catwalk around the tower toward us yelling, "Come here you little brats!"

We ran too. But the other way. When he went one way, we went the other. We could see he was annoyed and very mad trying to catch us. He was always on the wrong side of the tower from us, or we were always on the right side, or something like that.

Now there was a big crowd down in the yard. They were cheering at us and the guard was getting very mad, saying many things us kids maybe should not hear him say.

But the fun stopped after a bunch of soldiers came to the rescue of the guard. We were taken into custody.

Sitting on a bench outside the camp director's office, David told me, "Don't say anything, except give them your name and number."

"What number?"

"You know, the one we all got when we was evacuated."

"But I forgot dat damn number," I said.

"Oh well, just give them any number, they are really dumb," David said.

"Oh, Miyako, why? You could have fallen from that tower and hurt yourself and your friend. You gave everyone a fright. How should we punish you? They could have put the two of you in the stockade."

"But Mom, we didn't get hurt. It was wonderful. We were free. Free to see the whole camp an lots more. It was so great up there seeing all the barracks, animals, train tracks and lots of buildings and other blocks and ..."

"Quiet! That is just enough! Every day you will come straight home from school. From now on there will be plenty to keep you busy and out of trouble. You will soon be nine years old. You should act like that all grown-up girl you always say you are," Mom said.

Us kids were glad Mom and Dad started talking again. At the block meeting everybody was happy about the problems of the regular and the militant school. The chairman of our block said that the students were allowed to attend both the regular school in the mornings and the militants' classes on Japanese culture in the afternoon. So there would be no confusion about what classes we chose to attend and we would not miss regular school credits either way. The chairman thanked Mom and other mothers who helped work out the problems. I was so proud because Mom was given lots of cheers and handshakes by everyone.

Tomiko decided that after school she would take classes in flower arranging and tea ceremony.

"I'm trying to learn some more Japanese language an to write in hiragana script, but it's very hard. Some of the little kids really catch on fast. I might go see some of the other extra classes if I get time, but just don't want to hurt my school work," I told Mom and Dad.

One night I awoke suddenly. I heard someone in our apartment. A flashlight was shown right in my face by a guard or soldier. I screamed. He was very big and I cried and got under the covers.

Dad came right up to him and yelled at him to, "get out!" He pushed Dad who fell down. He told Dad to bring Michio outside. It was a camp security guard. He said, "He comes with us, now! He is to be questioned, he should be returned if he has done nothing."

Dad brought Michio outside and he left with the guard. He did not return for some time. Our parents tried to talk to the security people about coming in the apartment and asked what had Michio done, but they would not tell us. They said it was none of our business and warned us not to complain or organize any protests.

"Oh Dad, can't we get locks or something so they can't just come in and wake us and scare us?" I asked. "I can't sleep now."

"Let's switch beds and I will keep Michio's baseball bat with me. Just let one of those guys come in again and wham-o," Tomiko said.

"Oh no, please, you will end up in the stockade too." Mom said.

All we learned was that Michio was supposed to be part of the militants group, but nothing more.

"Well, the camp administration finally wakes up to what the militants are doing, as usual reacting very thoughtlessly, blindly and crudely. They really don't know how to respond to anything, except to retaliate blindly against innocent internees," Dad said.

"Michio had been implicated as one of the activists, but we don't know any more than that," Dad said.

All we ever found out was that Michio had refused to answer any questions about the militants' activities or give any information about his friends who were also in the stockade. Dad and other parents asked to meet with the camp administration.

"We asked if there would be a hearing or information concerning the arrests of our sons and daughters. We were given no answers," he said.

Every time the families tried to visit the stockade the gates were locked. At first we were able to wave at those in the stockade, but then large sheets of plywood were put on the fence to block everyone from seeing or waving to anyone in the stockade.

"Mom, Dad, when Tomiko and me tried to visit where Michio is we could not see him or anyone in the stockade. Big boards blocked the fence and we were told to go home by the guards," I cried. "Will we ever to see him?"

The next week security guards came in to the mess hall and questioned several of our neighbors. It scared us when they stopped near where we were eating. As they left one guard turned and pointed to Dad. "I know you people, watch yourselves! You could just as easily be keeping company with your nasty son."

Dad said nothing. He just looked at the guard. I was scared, I thought something was going to happen, but the guard walked away with the other guards. He was the same one who took Michio.

Finally some good news came. We all learned that an attorney from San Francisco, Mr. Wayne Collins, had been visiting the camp on many matters. When he heard about the stockade and all the arrests, he immediately threatened to go to court to close the stockade as being illegal. He was one of the ACLU attorneys from San Francisco who had opposed the internment.

Later the attorney did get the stockade closed, but not before many more inmates were locked up.

One day Tomiko said, "Mom, Michio is here, but someone shaved his head like the marching and singing guys. Michio, are you gonna renounce?"

"No, no, quiet, the guys did that where I was, but don't tell anyone. I didn't want to do that, besides I'm not old enough, just 17. But we have to keep quiet. I have been friendly with many of the guys. They are not bad, they mean well. There could be spies anywhere, the administration or the militants or others in the neighborhood. That is how come I was taken for questioning. I spoke up saying that some of the guys had good points. The camp security wanted me to tell them about my friends and other, but I said nothing. I would not rat on anyone, even if I knew anything. They kept dividing us up and trying to get us to give information. I would not say anything. They really were not pleased so they screamed and pushed us around. Quite a few of those also taken for questioning were beat up and tortured. I know the security guys liked to do that, all smiles," he said.

I stared for a long time at my brother and began to hug him and cried, "Oh, please be careful, we will be careful too. We want you home with us. We love you and I do most."

We got more good news, the family had received mail from Eichi.

"Look, I got this little one," I said, "It's a V-Mail. It sez he was wounded but he is OK now. He does not say where he is but that he can speak to people he met when his company liberated their village. That they speak the same language as our neighbors in San Francisco."

"Oh, I know," replied Tomiko, "I bet he is in Italy somewhere. He means the Desparis' who lived next door in the City."

"They often spoke Italian," Michio added.

The news of Eichi getting wounded was upsetting for us all, but mostly for Mom. "Oh dear, I hope we will learn more," she said, crying. We all tried to comfort her.

Two days later we received some very sad news, one of our uncles was killed during the same fighting Eichi was in. He was Mom's younger brother. Uncle Fred. She fainted. Between tears and grief and reviving Mom, Dad told Michio, Tomiko and me: "Oh, you two must write to your cousin Teri and Mom's sister, your aunt, they will be needing much comfort and love. We should send all of our letters together."

"Why so much bad news? Is it always like this in war time?" I asked Dad. He just shook his head, but did not answer.

In late March I came home from school with sad news, "Two of my best friend's parents are going to be sent to Japan with others in the camp. Dad, please, can you talk to their parents? My friends don't want to go to Japan. David is very upset and Rika was crying and sick about traveling. Neither has ever been to Japan, they are afraid."

"There is right now nothing we can do if their parents have renounced. Besides, those, like us, who oppose renunciation, have been threatened. We still cannot openly talk against it. We must be very quiet and remain neutral, but you can comfort them. They probably both need close friends more than ever," he said.

"Also, some who have renounced have been told by the militants that they cannot change their minds, even if that is not true. My boss at one of the coops has already been beaten for speaking against renunciation. Michio is right, there are spies who will continue to report to the militants. Other spies are working for the camp administration. We are caught between various factions," Dad added.

News came that the FBI and the justice department would be holding hearings and questioning those who have renounced. They will determine if some actually knew what they were doing when they gave up their citizenship. Including those who, after having renounced, had changed their minds and sought a reversal.

"Isn't our citizenship really valuable? That's what we are

told in school and what you guys have said?" I asked at our family meeting.

"Yes, of course, Kitty, you know that, but there is now still much hysteria and intimidation of all of us in camp. These things are not easy for anybody," Dad answered.

"Hopefully we can change all that someday. Just think, if the government had not given into the bigotry, hate and hysteria and had left us alone we could have helped win the war sooner. Now it has to foolishly pay extra time, personnel and money to continue to lock up innocents and falsely deport other Americans continuing the grief and hardship we have all been enduring," he added.

In late spring, many militants were transferred out of Tule Lake by the justice department and sent to DOJ internment camps. Including some of those with families who were sent to a WRA internment camp in Texas. The rumors were that those who continued to take part in the morning musters, such as marches and other nationalistic (Japanese) activities, would be sent to similar camps, now run by the Department of Justice. But those families who were transferred to the WRA internment camp in Texas had pending appeals of their possible deportation to Japan, including their children.

A week later Michio was again arrested by the camp security.

"We don't know anything about the charges as usual. We cannot even receive any information," Mom said.

She was very upset and did not stop crying, even when we

all went with other neighbors to protest the arrests of their sons and daughters. We knew that none were members of the militant groups.

"He is not an activist," Mom kept repeating to the camp security and several departments of justice persons. They just stared at Mom and the other neighbors, saying nothing.

"Dad, Mom, why don't they answer anyone's questions and our protests?" Tomiko asked.

"Because we are all the same to them. We are all those they branded since the start of the internment as being disloyal. The truth is that none of us here in Tule Lake camp are disloyal. They are in truth obliged to keep up the façade and the lie of internment. They could not even now afford to admit their wrong doings," Dad said.

"Now the family has lost another brother. Why? I wish there was something to keep him with us. I love him and am missing him already, it's not right," I said.

I thought back to when Dad had participated in the strikes and was locked in the stockade. I began shivering and left the apartment. Would Dad be taken away next? I whispered to little Buddha that afternoon. I hoped to myself that I was saying the right thing.

I told Lord Buddha, "I don't really know how to speak to you. I'm so worried. They took our Michio away again. Am afraid they might take Dad or even Mom too. Those guys are so bad it is hard to know what will happen. It is so hard to think, or say anything more."

My eyes were so filled with tears I could barely see little Buddha. "Oh Lord Buddha, I am just so afraid an feel so bad. Mom is feeling very upset and crying a lot. We are all more alone now."

Someone called to me, but I ran the other way. I was crying and running, running until I ran into someone. Not looking up to see who it was I got loose and kept running until I reached a fence, and began kicking and hitting it until I could not breathe. I just down. I was tired and looked out in to the fields for a long time. My stomach said I was hungry. I saw a mess hall line, and followed others. Afterwards I stepped outside. It was sunny, bright and warm. I started walking and felt happy no one knew or talked to me. Soon I found our school. It was not a school day, but the classroom was open and quiet. I got to my desk and began drawing. I made a picture of the camp. Remembering what we saw from the guard tower.

Some things had made me happy seeing the camp differently from the tower but then I remembered Michio now gone and Mom crying. I felt jittery and angry. The pencil I had was very thick and easy to draw big hard lines. I pushed it hard on the paper, making very dark places and deep groves in the drawing paper. I put stick people lying around the yard like I remembered seeing people from the tower. I drew until my wrist and arm ached from pressing so hard.

I asked myself. "Was anything good? What about the scary things that wouldn't go away? I can't remember when things were better. Can't we go home, please," I asked, talking to myself, a little out loud. Alone, no one could hear me, "Dad is not happy, and I am worried about Mom.

I try to remember some of Grandmother's music I loved. Good thoughts and happy times. What happened? I forgot all of it, an even our nice little garden. I can't feel or see our home."

Suddenly I was in the big park between the trees. Little water falls, flowers and soft grasses. Birds singing, tinkling of wind chimes and sounds of children playing. I wanted to dance. Looking around, I saw no one. The grass smelled good, it was soft on my feet. Again I heard the children laughing.

"Oh that is nice, I'll go play with them...but I can't find them and maybe I can't be here. It's dark and cold."

All the pleasant sounds went away. I could not hear, touch or see anything. I tried calling, I couldn't. Scared, alone and crying I was lost and afraid.

I did not remember leaving the schoolroom, but found myself on the floor next to my bed. Light was coming in between the cracks in the walls of the next-door apartment. A neighbor was talking. Still in my clothes, I got up and quietly went to our apartment door. Everyone was asleep. Pushing it open, I was met by the nice cool night air. Standing on the porch I stared into the star-filled night.

Whispering, so as not to disturb the night I asked: "Are you little stars so far away like me, lonely? Or like comets that keep going somewhere. Maybe like us, never allowed to go home?"

Staring at the stars, I got dizzy. Afraid I was going to fall into the glittering sky. I shuddered and stopped, trying to hold on to something. "Oh no, wait, I don't care if I fall into all the sky and stars, not now, I do not care anymore," I told myself.

I heard my friend the train, his lonely whistle. He was going somewhere in the night, farther and farther away until I could no longer hear his sad cry. I felt bad and cried to myself.

Something flashed in my eyes. I woke to the sun peeking between the next barrack, winking at me. Someone had draped a wool blanket over me. I was lying on the porch. A rooster said it was morning.

"Come Kitty, let's get something to eat," Dad spoke, smiling down at me.

I was happy and relieved to see him. I hurried to grab his hand.

"It's kind of early isn't it?"

"Yes, but don't worry, we'll find something."

The mess hall was almost deserted, except for the sounds of morning workers. Dad found some hot rolls and coffee. "Here, have a cup with me, it'll wake you, put some butter on these."

"Is it OK? I never had coffee before."

"Sure, just blow on it like tea and taste it slowly."

I was so excited and happy to be there with him that I

forgot everything that had made me sad and angry. Not even thinking about where we were, in camp, or how long we had been away from home. The coffee, warm and friendly, even if it tasted different, was good. I felt close to everything and everyone.

"Oh good, Kitty, you ate both rolls, you must have been hungry. Now let's get some breakfast."

"Thanks Dad, are you guys mad at me? I didn't come home for a long time last night and missed supper."

"No, of course not, it's nice you are here now."

"Are they going to take you away too?"

"No, I don't think they are mad at me or suspect me of anything. They know I opposed the militants, but we still must keep that to ourselves and stay alert, they are unpredictable. I am talking to one of the legal assistants acquainted with that attorney in San Francisco who helped us and others get the stockade closed. He might be able to help your brother and others were taken away, as well as all those who were pressed to renounce and have not been allowed to change their minds. But that is also a secret, we cannot tell anyone."

"Michio wants to be drafted, even if he will miss you and Mother and Tomiko. He does not feel he has much choice. He may be able to eventually join Eichi. What do you think?"

"Gee Dad, some guys won't like that, but what about Mom, how is she going to feel?"

"Well, for now, let's not tell her. Any more news will just upset her and she is upset enough."

"I promise Dad, I hope he is OK. I hope Mom will feel better. I sure love her and not want anything to happen to her. Thanks Dad, I love you."

On the way to school I remembered Dad, our, meeting and drinking my first coffee. I was happy. I had tears in my eyes and felt so grown up, just like my brothers and sister. Like I was no little kid anymore. It was a strange feeling, I was important now, even though I was still so short, but growing more.

In early April 1945 our teacher interrupted the regular class work. She seemed nervous and stuttered as she told the class, "I am very sorry to tell you that President Roosevelt has passed away. I don't know who has a radio so you might wish to inform your parents if they have not already heard the sad news."

One girl asked. "Didn't he help get us locked up? My parents thought he was going to help us once."

Miss Hart said nothing. I didn't know what to think. My parents had voted for him and said he helped us long ago when we were in Hawai'i when the economy was bad. Yet we couldn't understand when he got us locked up. Then he later approved of the law the congress made that allowed some Nisei to renounce their citizenship. Dad said that law was also unconstitutional and would hurt many of us for a very long time before anything might change.

About two months later when Tomiko and me returned

home from school Mom was crying. We tried to ask her, but she would not answer us, continuing to cry. We asked Dad.

"We lost our home in San Francisco," he answered.

"But why?" we asked.

"Well, it's very complicated. Because all our money was partially frozen, we were unable to pay on some of our mortgage. We were never given any warning, so we cannot return there and we don't know if we can recover any of our stored property or family money or somehow recover anything of what we have lost."

"You mean all our things that were stored are gone, lost?" Tomiko asked.

"They seem to have been lost or stolen. The people who were managing and renting out the home including making other house payments for us are missing. We have not been able to contact anyone. The government people and the WRA have not answered our letters, they are very slow to respond or do anything. So many others have also lost what was left to trusted people when we were interned. Now like them, we have no idea if we will recover anything," Dad concluded.

Tomiko and me hugged Mom and attempted to console her and ourselves. There were countless personal family items from many decades of our family that we may never see again. That night and for some days we fell silent. We could not talk about our loss. A big part of our lives was gone.

We were not alone. At the next block meeting, other families related about their losses. News was that many thousands of families who were wrongly evacuated lost property. During their absence, others had been taken advantage of by those they trusted.

One neighbor spoke for all of us, "All we have left, besides ourselves, are our memories."

One day when Tomiko and me returned from school Dad told us. "You girls will have to help your Mother. The doctor says she has had a nervous breakdown and must have complete rest. She may have to go to the hospital. From now on one of you will have to stay with her at all times."

We had all been worried about Mom because she stopped working in the mess and was not going to the teachers and block meetings. I remember that after we went to school she went back to bed, but I didn't know that she had not got up for noon meals and she sometimes was still sleeping when we got home.

"She has been so quiet and has hardly talked to us," Tomiko said. "And she stopped visiting the neighbors, we should have seen all those things happening. Mom has not been herself," Tomiko added.

With Eichi in military hospital overseas, Michio still in the justice department camp in New Mexico, and then her brother, our uncle, lost in the War, and all the misery of these years locked up. All of that had made Mom sick. It was so much for her and unfair. I also felt bad because of the times recently when I was not a very nice girl.

Tomiko tried to explain to me how Mom just took so much all on herself. "She has been very depressed. The doctor said we have to just be with her, let her know we care and love her. I don't know what else to tell you. Dad is also very quiet and unhappy now," she said.

I didn't know anything about depression. I asked Miss Hart. "Well, Kitty, it's said to be a mood change, but I am really not qualified to say much. From what you tell me about what you and your family has experienced with your mother, it could be that she is depressed. But as I said, someone who is qualified, a doctor, should explain that to you. I had wondered why we had not seen her in a while. We do miss her. From what I have heard, she needs all the love and caring you can give her," Miss Hart concluded.

She hugged me and said how sorry she was and hoped Mom would get better.

When Dad was away at work, each of us would miss some school to stay with her. One nearby neighbor was also able to help.

"How could we have helped her before she got so ill?" I asked Tomiko?

"I don't know, I feel bad and also wonder what we all could have done?"

I sat in silence, tears filling my eyes. Asking, did I make her ill? What could I have done better? Remembering what Grandmother and others had said about *ganbare*, "To keep going and holding together when it seems as if there is no sign of hope. Great inner strength." But I sat there so still and saddened.

When Dad came back I asked, "What can I do, I'm only nine? What you guys said about having *ganbare*, how do I hold on, everything seems so mean and sad? It should not have happened to Mom."

"Kitty, its everybody, all of us together. We have something more valuable, ourselves. That means the entire family, including those family members elsewhere. We must not to forget that as a family we will hold and support each other as well as your Mom. So we can all survive together. Now let's write many letters to your brothers and relatives. Being miles from each other means nothing to an entire family. We have now lots to do and no time to worry, regret, or feel sorry for ourselves."

That night I could not sleep until very late. I still thought about Mom. Asking over and over if I could have done something different and better. How happy she had been when we were all together in San Francisco. She loved the garden at home, a home that might not be there anymore.

Did anyone take care of it? Will we get to visit someday? Now I am really mad, but not so afraid. Yeah, mad at all that happened and for so long. Everyone was right, we did nothing wrong, it's all the fault of the prejudiced people and those who don't care in the government. But I still don't know them, and when are they going to stop everything and leave us alone? I would never do that to them. Lock someone up because of their ancestry. Just crazy, I'm going to make sure that it never happens anymore to anyone else. They have got to know this is America.

I remember when Mr. Adachi had trained all those little birds. He fed them and we talked to them and played with them, but they were never locked up. They were free because he trusted them and they trusted him. Those birds didn't care who our ancestors are. We trusted people, why could not all others trust us?

After school when I did not have to stay with Mom I visited the little Buddha. I whispered to him about Mom and how I felt. I was scared and did not want anyone else to know what was happening in our family. "Please Lord Buddha, help Mom get better and get happy again. We all love her. Thank you."

During the spring and into the summer of 1945 things began to quiet down in the camp. Many more militants had been sent to internment camps. Marching and other such activities had gradually stopped. More students were attending the regular classes, though some cultural classes were still being held which everyone appreciated.

In early August we all heard horrible and awful news. Hiroshima. Many neighbors and relatives came from there. The pictures in newspapers showed nothing but blackened acres of city streets and blocks.

"There was nothing but a few shells of buildings. I had been there and remember the thousands of places that now show nothing, and thousands of people burned up," a neighbor said.

It was too much for many to view and face. Many of our friends and neighbors with relatives there became sick.

"The pictures show that almost no one survived in that beautiful city. I cannot believe it," cried another.

"Why did they kill everyone? The kids, parents, all gone. People just like us," I was crying with everyone.

"Why did they have to use a bomb like that? An atom bomb, they said. All those were civilians, innocents. What did that prove? What happens now?" Another asked. "Will there be more? I am ashamed, that was so wrong," Dad said. "America did that? Our country did that?"

Within days there came the news of Nagasaki. Another atom bomb, more upon more died within one moment. Besides those two cities, tens of thousands of people in other cities perished from being fire bombed that blackened thousands of neighborhoods and farms. Those not immediately killed eventually starved to death.

About that time we all became aware of a bigger problem in the camp. Overnight there was panic among most of those citizens who had renounced.

Dad said, "The report of the justice department hearing has been announced. Almost all who renounced have been notified that they are to be deported. The original decisions have been accepted. So many wished to reverse those decisions that we know were hastily made under a climate of hysteria, intimidation, duress or misinformation. Many of our neighbors are now considered enemy aliens by the authorities, and are to be deported. They will not be allowed to change their minds and reverse the renunciation of their citizenship," Dad said.

"Does it mean that some of our friends and neighbors won't be able to stay? How can they live in Japan, it is in ruins? It was not their fault. That is just more punishment. Can't anything be done?" Tomiko asked Dad.

"Not by us, they will have to seek outside help. But now it will not be easy," Dad answered.

A special committee was formed. They asked the JACL for assistance. But the JACL again turned them down. Fortunately one person was available who had assisted other inmates on matters involving the camp administration and the government. Wayne Collins, the San Francisco attorney, and a small number of other American Civil Liberties Union attorneys from San Francisco began to assist the distressed families and other inmates seeking the reversal of their renunciation of citizenship.

"I just hope that they can help. It is our friends and neighbor's only chance now," Dad said.

"I heard that when we were first interned that the national ACLU had approved of the internment of US citizens in the concentration camps in early 1942," Tomiko said.

"Yes, only the San Francisco ACLU chapter refused to endorse that position," Dad said. " That one attorney, Mr. Collins, and their committee will attempt to assist those families to escape deportation."

Unfortunately we much later learned that it would become a long and drawn out crisis that would not be solved for many years. Deportations still took place, and most were found to be illegal. Many were not able to regain their citizenship until after having been sent to Japan.

We also learned, unfortunately, those who were deported were often unwelcome when they arrived there, because they were an added burden to those Japanese who survived in a defeated country, where there was a lack of basic food and shelter to survive from day to day. Tens of thousands were starving in the majority of cities and in the countryside.

"Those that are being sent to Japan will have nothing to eat or shelter. They and all of us here have been further abandoned by our government, so unforgiving and tenacious in its lack of human decency, responsibility and empathy toward its own citizens," Dad concluded.

In the fall, Dad asked me and Tomiko, "Help me girls, we must get your mother ready. The doctors wish her to be examined. They fear she is not recovering, losing more weight and her health in general is now threatened."
We began crying, holding each other. We helped her with her things into one of the camp cars. She was hardly aware of us.

Waving goodbye, with tears in my eyes I asked dad, "Where will they take her? When can we visit? Dis is so awful."

"I am not sure, possibly one of the state hospitals where she can receive professional help. Let's us pray and hope she will recover." Dad answered. "I don't know when we can even visit. Sorry girls."

It would be a long time before we would receive any good news about Mom.

Many times we hugged Dad and tried to console him. It was so hard and miserable for him. I don't know how he had been able to keep going and take care of Tomiko and me.

"Is there anything more that can go bad?" I asked myself out loud, as if I could even have an answer. "Why did this happen? Why to us? We did nothing wrong."

I asked little Buddha. I told him all that had happened to Mom and a lot of our neighbors who were leaving for Japan. I cried and hoped that all I said was all right to say, "Lord Buddha, I know I don't know how to pray and ask for help. Please don't be tired of me. I am sure I complain too much. Please just forgive me."

The war had ended that September and everyone was talking about peace and the future. There were no celebrations. I don't think that after all that had happened we could be very happy. For us in camp, what did it matter? We were still locked up.

It was silence in the apartment. Dad was occupied with the committee's attempts to reverse the governmental decisions concerning deportations and release of those inmates interned elsewhere. Now there were only three of us.

"It's a different quiet, a different kind of loneliness. We got so many more people to worry about." I told Tomiko and Dad.

"I really miss Mom, but I don't know how I could have helped. And how much of it was my fault? What did I do that maybe help make her sick? Sometimes I don't think I came home soon enough and should not have complained about so much when she called. I didn't try hard enough to help and love her. I hope she forgives me, because I love her so much and miss her."

"Oh Kitty, no, we can't just fault ourselves," Tomiko said. "Mom would never wish that, no matter what. I don't believe she wants us to blame anyone."

"When she left in the ambulance she asked that we just take care of each other and continue to love ourselves," Dad said.

One lonely day I got very frightened and ran to Tomiko, "Tomiko, Tomiko, you gotta listen to me, I am much afraid and worried. I have a secret to whisper to you..."

"Oh, Kitty, is that all?" Tomiko laughed. "That's all right, not to worry, you just be happy. I do that and it's natural. You are just growing up. Soon you will be 10, and there are other secrets that I'll tell you. Unless, you already know about."

At first I didn't know what to say. Just stood there and said nothing for a while, then I said: "Oh, OK, I think I know, gee, thanks, it's really nice having a big sister to share secrets." We hugged and laughed. Tomiko for all our time together was the best and greatest sister in the world. She has always been there. I don't ever know if I can thank her enough.

One school day I asked Miss Hart, "With the war all over, how come we are still locked up?" Another student repeated the same question, and another. Soon almost the entire class was asking questions to our now bewildered teacher. She could not really give us any answers.

"I am so sorry and ashamed because nobody should have ever been evacuated in the first place. Why don't we all talk about going home because we know the camp will close very soon?"

"But where? We cannot go to our home, Dad says we lost it, everything," I cried, "We have no place to go. An Mom is very sick because of everything." There were tears in my eyes and I put my head on my desk and continued crying. I felt so bad and embarrassed for asking about da damn war and us.

Others started talking about their families' problems and worried about returning somewhere or anywhere. I was not the only one. Some too had lost their homes and loved ones.

Miss Hart had no answer. I think she was embarrassed. That was my fault. I started it. It was the beginning of our school year. The long war may have been over for the rest of school kids in the nation, but not for us, still interned, locked up in America.

That afternoon I again visited little Buddha. Whispering, I asked again, "Please Lord Buddha, help Mom to get well. She is in hospital, now we do not know where. She needs to be better. Mom has done nothing wrong. She is so very good and the best Mom. We are really alone now, the family. Our brothers are both away and we don't know where we are going to go if we can't go home? It is now all gone." I just sat there for what seemed to be a long time. I kept asking in my heart that the family come back together, my Mom, my brothers, everyone, please.

The sun was just setting when I saw Tomiko nearby. "Do you trust God? You best ask to get everybody out of this mess. I just don't know if I can trust. Look where we are now, we have nothing, just misery," she said. "We better go now, it's supper time."

That night I again had bad dreams. I was looking for everybody. They were all lost in a city I could not recognize. It didn't seem like San Francisco, not that I could remember. Nothing looked familiar and there was no daylight, just darkness.

I cried for Mom. I was asking for my Mom. There was no one there. I didn't know why I kept asking. I woke, realizing that no one was there. I heard that train whistle. It was still dark and I was glad to be awake. A lonely sound, it gave me shivers, but after all the time in camp, I liked it. It seemed to cry like we felt. It was sadness going by in the night. So far away going somewhere and then I was sleeping again.

That morning when I woke I looked around for Mom. Again realizing she was gone, I cried some more.

Did Mom get sick because we didn't love her enough? Maybe I need to write another letter to her. I hope she can read our mail. She had just lain there so quietly and hardly doing anything before she left. Was it my fault? I didn't always sit with her when we went to the mess hall. But now what can I do? We better not lose anyone else. I hope Michio can come back from New Mexico and Eichi visit soon. He's going to have to help Dad so we can be a family again.

The next day Dad received some good news. Eichi was coming. He had been released from the army hospital and would be able to visit the family. I felt really good.

"I hoped for Eichi and now he is coming home—well, not really home—but we will have more family for a little while. So, Tomiko, maybe it works to hope and pray. Someone does listen all the time and knows it hasn't been easy," I told her.

"Oh yeah, an we got a letter from Michio, he got a draft notice so he is going to enlist in the army. That means he gets out of that internment camp. Maybe he will come here to visit?" Tomiko said.

More families moved out of our block. At first just a few were able to resettle, and then some were traveling to Japan. My friends and classmates began to slowly disappear.

"Oh David, am awful sorry you got to leave, I'm going to miss you so." I stood there near his family's apartment, with tears in my eyes as his family finished packing.

"Yeah, me too," he said, "will really miss you, but we did have some good fun. They sure went crazy when we climbed that darn tower. Am not going to forget that."

We laughed and hugged each other. Later I watched as his family passed through the camp gate. I kept waving, David waving back, until he was out of sight. It took so long for them to reach that gate. I just did not want him to leave. Tears were again welling up in my eyes and began to feel very sad.

I thought to myself, he was my really good and best friend, really good, but I didn't tell him, I should have. I think I am just too shy. I just don't know much about boyfriends and that kind of thing.

Now he will be thousands of miles away in Japan. I should have talked more to him. I will miss him, really will. Honest. Now he is gone, really gone. Maybe I could see him sometime again, I hoped. Another most empty feeling. Not quite like when Grandma died, more like something I didn't understand.

It was raining one Sunday when Tomiko and I returned from breakfast. "Dad's not here yet, where could he be?" I asked.

Tomiko screamed, "It's Eichi! He's with Dad, he has his uniform on! Quick, let them in before they get too wet."

That day, though dark and dreary outside, became one warm, festive and bright place in the family apartment. If only Mom had been home.

Eichi seemed to know how we were feeling, "Hey you girls, cheer up, Mom would not want to see you two looking so glum. She's here in spirit," he said.

We finally relaxed and soon started continually asking our biggest brother questions, and exchanging hugs. It was late before anyone went off to bed. I felt happy and was able to sleep and dream nice thoughts for the first time in a while.

When day came, Tomiko and I both wanted to take Eichi to our classes. We were so proud and insisted he keep his uniform on so we could show him off. He was continually introduced as our "Go-For-Broke" brother. ("Go-For-Broke", the unit motto of the 100th Battalion and the 442nd Regimental Combat Team. Nisei volunteers from the concentration camps, and Hawai'i).

"An he is a hero, our brother," we kept telling everyone we met.

"Now things are different," I told myself. No more does Eichi kid me about being so little. Unlike the soldiers here at camp, he helped win the war. Those guys here did nothing but scare, intimidate and order us around.

Dad asked me if I still was reluctant to say the pledge in the classroom when it came my turn. "Well, we are still locked up and not treated equal like the pledge says."

"Kitty, remember that thousands of young men, like your brother Eichi, were also locked up, but were still willing to fight under that flag for something greater that they believed in. They represented all of America. The whole nation, and many gave their lives for what we all believe, freedom and democracy, for all of us."

Eichi told us some of the many things he and his comrades had experienced. One incident he said was important for us to sometime find more about. "You see all of us were not the only persons locked up during the war for false reasons. Some of our units helped liberate Dachau. It was also called a concentration camp. You will learn more about it sometime soon. Remember, when we received a number for the entire family when we were interned? There were many millions of another peoples who were tattooed with their names on their arms and shoulders. Incarcerated in camps because of their ancestry and religion. And very few survived, most were murdered. It is being known as the "Holocaust" and we need to learn everything that happened over there. That is another reason we signed up, to be involved, to fight for what we all believe, democracy. We were not the only people to suffer due to our ancestry and discrimination," he concluded.

Just before the New Year, 1946 Dad had some good news. "By the end of January we will be able to leave Tule Lake camp. We have found a place to live in San Francisco. The WRA (War Relocation Authority), those who ran the camps, are helping us for a change," he said.

"It's in a housing project, but just a small apartment. One of you girls may have to stay with your aunt Loretta in Southern California. Cousin Teri would be glad to see either of you girls," he added.

"But what about Mom? And Michio?" Tomiko asked.

Dad explained, "We hope that by then we will know more about your mother. Hopefully she can return to us. We must keep praying for her to recover. These years have been so difficult for her. Eichi will be visiting her in a few days. He can let us know how she is doing. Michio might also see us later. We don't know when he starts with the army. At least he will be out of that damn Department of Justice internment camp in New Mexico.

The day we leave this camp, each of us will be given $25.00 along with a travel ticket. Which I think is very strange. You see, each convict who is freed from prison is given the same payment along with a travel ticket For added insult, here is a little booklet on How to Make Friends and How to Behave in the Outside World. You will find it most pathetic and amusing. They just do not cease in their insults and stupidity," Dad concluded.

"So now they are saying that we are considered convicted criminals and are not admitting that they lied to us," Tomiko said.

I told everyone that I still had a dilemma, "I'm mad at somebody, those guys we never met. They are so ignorant. They knew nothing about any of us. But locked us up because of our ancestors. For just being different from themselves. It now seems so silly. Maybe what Mr. Omori and others said, that all prejudice was not really so important to be concerned about. Not to let it get us down because we are so much bigger than those who hurt us. That it was just what happened, *sho-ga-nai,* he called it— not something like fate, but nothing we could not do anything about.

I still love America, even if we had to go to the camps. But really still would like to know just how we can pledge allegiance to the flag when not everything the pledge says is true. That some of us are not equal and not have equal justice and liberty. I am going to think more about what

Dad said and Eichi did, but also promise to do what I can so nothing that happened to all of us will be repeated.

If things had been different we could have helped like Eichi and other soldiers who were allowed to help America during the war. I guess I figured something out, even if it was not really important. I am still an American citizen, even if some people think differently. They were just wrong and mistaken. I can even feel sorry for them now. I still don't see others as being different. Like those kids in school, they looked the same as Tomiko and me.

Maybe I will never see any difference. I think that is good. That is what I believe. I am just me. That is all I want to be, me."

The last day of school Miss Hart asked me to stay after class. She had a drawing I had made and she seemed very concerned. It was the one drawn in heavy pencil, when I saw the camp from the guard tower. Buildings, barracks and surrounding fields were colored black, and the sky very dark. Stick people lying down, and in each of their eyes were crosses, very sad to look at.

"Kitty, what is this about? It seems very depressing. And what are all the people doing? And why did you draw them like stick people. You are a good artist and know how to draw people better than that, not like simple stick people, as kindergarteners do. Why?"

"It's about the camp. They are all sad and sick and not real. They are not allowed to be real people. They don't like the camp or anything else. It's not a place for anyone, ever."

"Well, what about how you feel? Are you in the picture somewhere?"

"I don't know. When we climbed that tower we were happy seeing everything. It was like being free for just a little while. I tried to tell Mom that. Maybe I didn't put me in it, I don't know, maybe I'm there too, I can't answer. You can have it, I don't want it, just want to forget and go home."

"Well, thank you, Kitty. I will keep it as one of my memories of Tule Lake. You were a very excellent and very sensitive student. I am honored to have known you."

She hugged me and we said goodbye. As I left the classroom and Miss Hart, I began crying to myself.

One very pleasant day I found myself wandering along the fence near the apartments. Staring into the distant hills, I told myself, "This could have been a really nice place, it sure has pretty fields and hills, oh so green. Many, many kinds of birds, they sound so happy. I wonder what they are singing about? I like the different wild flowers and wish I could send some to Mom. She would love to see them. Now I don't want to kick the fence anymore. It's easy to forget it is even there. I might visit this place someday, just not now or for a long, long time. Could we please, stop things from ever happening to others like happened to us and have everyone trust each other? Just hope I will be less afraid when we leave. It will sure be different being sort of free. Just maybe a little scared. I still don't like ever having to think about that ancestry thing. Out there, will those people see me differently still?"

One morning Dad called me. He had something to give me. It was the little Buddha. "Your friend Mr. Izawa in the next block wanted you to take care of it when he left. He is a very good wood carver. Did you know he was such an excellent artist?"

"Oh, I missed him, he must have returned to Hawai'i. He was from there. I wanted to say goodbye to him. I'm sorry I missed him," I said.

"No," Dad said, "He went to Japan with the others, he wanted to find some of his relatives who hopefully survived the war."

"Oh no, no, he was from Hiroshima." I began to cry. That was very upsetting and I was shaking. Dad held me close, trying to calm me. After a while I relaxed.

"What is he going to do now? I hope he finds someone left, it's so sad and all wrong." Dad shook his head in silent reply.

Again, there were tears in my eyes. I said, "I guess he loved me, he always talked to me. I wasn't afraid of him. He was not like some others. I did not have a chance to tell him thanks for letting me talk to Lord Buddha. Maybe I could write to him?"

I held the little Buddha and ran back out into the yard. Not knowing really where to go or why. I felt happy and sad. I started crying, when I reached the fence. Still holding Little Buddha, crouching down, I leaned against it and stared into the way-off fields.

I was soon in the great park near where we had lived. Looking for our home and garden, but again I was lost, unable to find anything. "Oh, it's all gone." I told myself.

When I woke, still clinging to the little Buddha, I looked at it and whispered, "Oh thank you. Thank you for all those nice friends and you. Soon we can leave camp. I got some answers, some wisdom, and even if I don't know all the questions. And Lord Buddha, thank you for helping me see things better. You helped me see Love in everything, even those in camp who we were afraid of. They were also our neighbors. I promise to take good care of you. Maybe there will be others who will see you and you can be of help. But please, I am very scared, very scared going. I am afraid not knowing what might happen to us. Help me please."

For days to follow, time passed quickly and almost deliberately. The New Year started and school was over for Tomiko and me. Every day there were more empty tables in the mess hall. The laundry was now silent and familiar faces were missing. The sounds of all kinds of activity were gone. I could hear myself think. It was strange and even lonely.

While everyone who remained was packing, I came to Dad and asked, "Dad, is it OK if everyone just calls me Miyako from now on? I'm kinda different now, a little older, a little bigger an it is my name, please."

"Oh Miyako, of course, that's your name and you are right. But tell me, you gave away Panda, didn't you?"

"Yeah, to Rika, she had to go to Japan with her family and

she was really sad, but happy to have Panda. She is going far away and Panda is nice to be with and hold. It made me happy, even if I will miss both. She was one of my best friends. And Dad, may I take my army blankets with?"

"Sure, but you used to complain about them being so scratchy. You still want them?"

"I'm used to them now, and they are good when it's cold. If we had not had them in Topaz camp, we might have frozen more than we did."

FAREWELL TO TULE LAKE

Then it came, that last day. We passed for the last time through the now unlocked gates of Tule Lake camp.

While we held each other close, Dad, Tomiko, and me, I glanced back at those long rows and rows of drab and gaunt barracks which began to fade as dust devils spun among now silent blocks and firebreaks, empty of almost everyone.

For a moment I thought we could hear children playing, a door slam, the crunch of gravel under marching feet, the faint echo of someone calling, then the momentary vision of someone running in fright and flight. Just as suddenly, there was the faint din of music I long forgot. I could not see. My eyes were blurry. I almost wanted to smile but I just could not be happy, even if we were outside the camp.

I was really scared to death and afraid of tomorrow.

———————————

Those remaining members of the family took their last steps onto the train, silently dragging luggage to their seats.

Fading thoughts of bad dreams. Four years of slow turmoil, a multitude of heartaches and reluctant imprisonment, undeserved, and lost in time.

A time out of the ordinary. A time in America.

-- Fil Kae

www.ingramcontent.com/pod-product-compliance
Lightning Source LLC
Chambersburg PA
CBHW062144280526
45788CB00001B/295